WORKING IN THE JETSTREAM

Tales from thirty years
flying as an airline steward

BRIAN LEARY

Published in Australia by Sid Harta Books & Print Pty Ltd,
ABN: 34632585293
23 Stirling Crescent, Glen Waverley, Victoria 3150 Australia
Telephone: +61 3 9560 9920, Facsimile: +61 3 9545 1742
E-mail: author@sidharta.com.au

First published in Australia 2023
This edition published 2023
Copyright © Brian Leary 2023
Cover design, typesetting: WorkingType (www.workingtype.com.au)

The right of Brian Leary to be identified as the Author of the Work
has been asserted in accordance with the Copyright, Designs and Patents Act 1988.

This book is copyright. Apart from any fair dealing for the purpose of private study, research, criticism or review, as permitted under the *Copyright Act 1968*, no part may be reproduced by any process whatsoever without the publisher's express written permission.

Brian Leary
Working in the Jetstream
Airlines—crew—passengers—anecdotes—travel
ISBN: 978-1-922958-14-3

pp260

ABOUT THE AUTHOR

Brian Leary was born in the southwest town of Temora, NSW, in 1936 and for the next twelve years lived in the Westminster Hotel, which was owned and run by his parents. They then moved to Sydney and Brian went to a trade school in Surry Hills for four years. After leaving school he undertook an apprenticeship in Fitting and Machining.

'As soon as I got my certificate, I left on a ship bound for England to see the world. I would ramble about all over the continent and England until I ran out of money and then do odd jobs before going walkabout again. At one point I secured a job at Ferrari's Motors and stayed there six months driving around England, then returned to Sydney in 1961 and to a recession.

'A retail whitegoods company employed me for the unsavoury job of repossessing appliances.

'By chance I saw an ad in the *Sydney Morning Herald* requiring three stewards for overseas service with Qantas Empire Airways.

'I applied ... there were over two thousand applicants and yes, I was one of the lucky ones, and over the next thirty years progressed up the ranks to Chief Flight Steward.

'I met thousands of VIPs in situations where you could sit and talk with them.

'When Gough Whitlam became prime minister, the chance fell my way to be his valet, touring all over Europe.

'During the Vietnam War, I was a volunteer, and from 1969 to 1971 flew as air crew, transporting troops and equipment into war zones.

'Then, I was involved in rescuing two hundred and fifty orphan children from Saigon during the bombardment and subsequent fall in 1975. For this, I was invited to be on Mike Munro's TV program, *This Is Your Life*.

'Retirement came in a rush and flying was over. I had tuition in singing, culminating in the year 2000 singing in a small group of eleven in St Peter's Basilica in Rome to Pope John Paul II.

'With my beautiful wife, who worked at 2SM radio station (we were engaged on air), we took up dancing, and both have gold medals as champions.

'We have three children who all flight crew for the airline, with a whopping combined 118 years of service between us.

'My interest has always been in vintage cars that have come and gone. At the moment it is a Studebaker and a 1928 fire engine.

'I enjoy reminiscing about my adventurous life.'

Disclaimer and Acknowledgements

The names of some people and places in this book have been changed to protect not only the innocent but also the guilty. An account of the following anecdotes has been included in a fellow author's work, when years ago in a crew's rooms I shared the stories with him: *Change the baby*; *Captain Crap*; and *Mal's wig*. However, he wasn't there — but I was, so recollections of those events are mine alone.

Please note that a lot of these stories happened before aviation 'knuckled down to business' by making far stricter rules. There is no way the majority of the events described in this book would be tolerated now. Restrictions, rules, antidiscrimination, equal rights, antiharassment, unions, customs regulations and management have all tightened the reins on errant behaviour. As with most things, this has taken a lot of the fun out of it.

The period about which I write was a hard-drinking, hard-working time, and service to the passengers was something not done out of duty alone, but undertaken out of pride in our job and the airline.

With thanks to Margaret Knowlden, Colin Burgess

Dedication

To my wife Annette,

and all the other crew wives at home acting as both mother and father,

keeping the family together until our return from overseas flights,

and to my tea-towel-waving mum.

Working in the Jetstream

Contents

Prologue	1
1. Santa	7
2. Stuck	9
3. Calypso Cola in Cairo	12
4. Crackers	14
5. Pea soup	16
6. Change the Baby	20
7. Have a Nice Day	21
8. A Good Day for Flying?	23
9. The Twenty-Pence Bargain	24
10. Len	25
11. Calamity	27
12. Sponsored by Coca-Cola	29
13. Mr Smooth	32
14. The lottery	34
15. Ricky	35
16. Give Them Nothing	38
17. Magic Word	39
18. Hong Kong	40
19. Passenger Comments	44
20. Shiners	45
21. Auckland PAs	46
22. Dobbers	47

23. Babylon	48
24. Little Nancy	49
25. The one-shoe shuffle	50
26. Two Little Words	50
27. Here It Is	51
28. Silhouette	52
29. Drop the Bridgestones	53
30. What Do You Do for a Crust?	54
31. Bouncy Bits	55
32. Uncommon Sense	57
33. The Motorbike Affair	58
34. Don't Feed the Convicts	59
35. Don't Feed the Dogs	61
36. Vera	61
37. Pickles	62
38. My Dad	63
39. The Camper	63
40. Dennis and the Love Letter	64
41. Rudi	65
42. Johno's One-and-only Call	67
43. Dangly Bits	68
44. Infernal Horn	69
45. Hitman	70
46. 472 years	71
47. Zeb's Last Fling	72
48. Learning the Age-old Game	73
49. Chamber of Fools	74
50. Hoppy's Shooters	75
51. Marian	79

52. Beach Shirts and Live Wires	84
53. Boy, Oh Boy — What a Lady!	86
54. Bay Rum and Mirror Man	88
55. My Goodbye	90
56. The Palmist	91
57. Happy Birthday, Cardboard Box Babies	97
58. Welcome to Vietnam	102
59. Cardboard Box Baby Reunion	104
60. Surviving Against All Odds	105
61. And Then the Sun Came Out	106
62. The Turtle	109
63. Customs	110
64. Lost Property	113
65. The Eleventh Commandment	114
66. Bluey	115
67. Out-of-control Controllers	116
68. One-way Horse Riding	117
69. Siddy	118
70. San Francisco (before Hank and Larry)	119
71. Lennie	121
72. Warts and All	122
73. Lunch with the Royals	122
74. The lecture	125
75. Head Gear and Ear Muffs	126
76. Gamblers	127
77. Jim	128
78. Caught with my pants down	130
79. Captain Crap	131
80. Ports	132

81. Brains in your Suitcase	133
82. It Takes All Types	134
83. Fence Wire and UFOs	139
84. Hotels We Stayed In	142
85. Welcome Aboard	146
86. I quit, So Can You	149
87. That's Hong Kong, Sir	150
88. Connie and Harry	151
89. Soup Kitchen and Hank and Larry	153
90. Race Day	155
91. Crews	157
92. The Gourmet Breakfast	158
93. Bolt Upright	161
94. Room 1306	163
95. Fun Flights	165
96. A Royal Hello	166
97. Rorting Roy	168
98. Room for Two	170
99. My Mate, Mick	177
100. World of Music	180
101. Not Bloody Going	183
102. Happy Birthday, Mrs O'Connor	184
103. Speech Therapy	185
104. Bunny's Foot	187
105. The Weekender	189
106. Lost and found — mainly lost	192
107. I Know the King	194
108. Cloud Nine	195
109. G'day, Mate	196

110. The Upgrade	198
111. Mal's Wig	200
112. Glamour in the Air	201
113. Soap	202
114. Irene	203
115. Shanty Hygiene	204
116. A Child's View	205
117. Calcutta (Kolkata)	206
118. Chicken or Beef	206
119. Free at Last	207
120. The Champion	209
121. Underpaid	210
122. Service with a Smile	210
123. Not Going	211
124. The Side Show	212
125. From Ties to T-shirts	213
126. The Yank	214
127. The Captain's PA	214
128. Red	215
129. Oh Ye of Little Faith	215
130. Lexie	216
131. Dawn Air-raid Siren	217
132. The Best Job in the World	217
133. Cabaret	218
134. Nicknames	219
135. Runway to Highway	220
136. Heinui and the La Fayette	220
137. The Dip	223
138. Moustaches	223

139. Hell on Earth	224
140. The El Paso	227
141. Gone	229
142. Chop, Chop	229
143. Haa Toro	230
144. My Little Trick	232
145. Dining in the Third World	232
146. The Hunter	234
147. The Upside-down Newspapers	236
148. Devastated	239
149. The End — but also the beginning	240

Prologue

've made it, I happily thought to myself as Mr Walton, the crew manager, shook hands and handed me my shiny metal wings for my uniform on graduation day. Six long months in the school (we called it the 'College of Knowledge') had taught me how to cook, address VIPs, give silver service, make fancy cocktails, demonstrate in-flight safety and give first aid. It was time to let me loose among the passengers.

Mr Walton was droning on yet again about being ambassadors to both the airline and the country. 'Never, never disgrace them. Dignity is a must,' he concluded. 'You are now ready to become a crew member in an enviable and very unique job that not only will take you to places you could until now only dream of, but you will see the funny, sad, surprising, unbelievable, stupid, incredible and fascinating things of life in your travels.'

He then came to the most important part we were all waiting for — the allocation of our first flight destinations on the magic carpet in the sky.

'Mr Armstrong,' Mr Walton said, looking over the top of his glasses and hesitating a second. 'New York.

'Mr Phillips — London.

'Mr Linder — Tokyo.

'Mr Georgeson — Hong Kong.'

I was leaning back in my chair, eyes closed, letting the words wash over me, smiling to myself while waiting for the big moment. Mr Walton droned on.

'Mr Jones — Johannesburg.

'Mr Leary — Biak.'

I shot bolt upright. *Did he say Biak?*

'Excuse me, Mr Walton, but did you say "Biak"?'

'Yes, Leary, Biak. You're on an engine exchange charter flight.

'Mr Young — Honolulu.'

'Excuse me again, Mr Walton, but what kind of aircraft am I flying on?'

'DC3,' he hissed at me.

Good Lord! While the rest of the school is jetting about on 707s to romantic places, I am on an egg-beater DC3 to wherever the hell Biak is. Marvellous, bloody marvellous. Nurse-maid to a reconditioned engine strapped down in the cabin.

When I got home that night from the graduation, Mum and Dad excitedly asked me where my first flight was to. 'Biak,' I bleakly replied.

'Where's that?' they both asked together.

'Search me,' I said, shrugging my shoulders. Mum got out the old blue school atlas and looked it up.

'Ah, here it is,' she said. 'Map 3, latitude 1°.00S, longitude 136°.00E.'

A dot off the coast of New Guinea on the Equator was going to be my first destination, with an eight-hour flight time ahead of me.

Back from the uneventful, boring Biak trip, I apprehensively approached the roster desk in the office at the airport. The cabin crew manager handed me my roster, saying, 'Brian, we have picked you out to do an historic flight.'

'Historic?' I murmured.

'Yes,' he continued. 'Bart Cummings is sending over four horses from New Zealand for the Melbourne Cup. It has never been done before. A world first.'

'Horses,' I whispered, looking at the manager for some trace of a smile, telling me it was a joke.

This time it was a Super Constellation, known affectionately to all aircrew as 'Connie'. The Connie, incidentally, was the first aircraft to be designed as a passenger plane; all other aircraft before it were either cargo or military planes converted for civilian use. We flew down to Auckland with the cabin full of cargo, as the interior had been stripped of seats and fittings. Early next morning they loaded the four magnificent horses wearing specially-made crash helmets, and suspended them in what appeared at first glance to be hammocks with four holes for their legs.

During the flight over to Melbourne, I got talking to the strapper and he told me out of the corner of his mouth to put money on *Even Stephens* for 'The Cup'. Not only did I put all my money on this horse, but I told everybody down at my local pub to do the same. On the following Tuesday afternoon, *Even Stephens* romped home by five lengths and I didn't have to buy a drink down at the pub for months.

By this time, I had run across most of my mates from the school, all talking about exciting places: Buckingham Palace, San Francisco cable cars, Tokyo nightclubs, Hong Kong shopping, and swaying palms on sunny beaches. All got a mention, and girls. My flights didn't rate a mention.

*

The roster clerk behind the counter called my name and I approached him saying to myself, *Please, please let it be a passenger service.*

'I'm sorry, mate,' he said, with a half-apologetic smile on his face. 'I didn't roster you for this.' Looking down at the roster sheet the words were blurred, except for 'monkey' charter.

'Monkeys,' I croaked.

I should explain that during the late 1950s and early 1960s there was a serious epidemic of polio in Australia, and the Commonwealth Serum Laboratories were frantically manufacturing a Salk vaccine to combat it. Monkeys were used as the incubators of the vaccine and were being brought from the jungles of Burma and Sumatra.

Even from a distance, as we walked across the tarmac to the 'Connie' parked well away from the old Singapore terminal, screeching coming from the inside could be heard. At twenty yards (eighteen metres) the stench hit us.

Ambassadors to the country, flashed through my brain.

'Good Lord, this is going to be living hell,' muttered Captain Clous (known as 'Santa') as we climbed the steel steps to the aircraft door.

The ground crew who had been minding the 'passengers' until we arrived, made a bee-line for the door, running from the smell so fast they could have been contenders for the hundred-yard sprint in the Olympics.

The technical crew hurried up to the flight deck, slamming the door and flicking on the air-conditioner. I stood rooted to the spot, looking down the length of the interior. Floor-to-ceiling cages had been bolted to the bulkheads on both sides of the cabin, crammed full of monkeys with bared teeth, all staring at me. A narrow passage had been left down the middle for access to the rear to feed the little blighters.

These lovable, pretty-faced, cuddly little monkeys greeted me with savagely revealed canines and high-pitched screeches as I made my way warily down the narrow passage. Later, I was to describe them as rotten, conniving, missile-throwing, stinking little bastards. The walk down the aisle was plainly asking for it, and only done as a last resort. Guess where the toilet was? The monkeys threw with deadly precision the only thing they had plenty of lying around, and it doesn't take an IQ of 200 to figure out what that was.

Ten hours, three minutes and six seconds later (not that we were counting), we landed back in Sydney on this flying zoo and it seemed more like a week. It was a race to get off, after the captain, that is. Nobody in the 'good old days' would dare get off before him. Kevin, the flight engineer, gave me a lift in his car to Sydenham Station. Neither of us could smell the dreadful odour in our clothes as we had become quite used to it.

The train pulled into the station when I suddenly realised that it was peak hour and jam-packed. Squeezing in with the crowd, the door closed and, before we had arrived at the next station, I had four square metres of space all to myself. The commuters were all pressed up against one another like fish bait, glaring at me in my almost new, now-soiled uniform. It was at this point my pride as an ambassador took a severe plunge and I hurriedly left with my suitcase at the very next station as soon as the door opened. The station was also crowded, so I spent an hour hiding behind a Lipton's Tea billboard, sitting on my case until the rush hour was over.

When I finally got home, the family were seriously considering whether they would let me into the house. Scrubbing furiously under the shower in the laundry, my crumpled uniform in a heap on the floor, I was sorely tempted to terminate my career with Zoo Airlines. I'm glad now that I didn't.

Brian Leary

1. Santa

The roster sheet had Hong Kong stamped on it and underneath it was written, *Aircraft type: Boeing 707.* At last! Being new and not knowing any crew yet, I didn't bother reading the crew names on the compliance sheet. But I did notice that Santa from the monkey charter was the captain and Alex Williams was the chief steward.

When we finally arrived at Hong Kong via Port Moresby and Manila, Alex did what most chiefs did for someone on their first trip — which was to show them around. Of course, it depended on the particular chief's idea of 'showing you around'. Some, the casinos, bars, race tracks; others knew the strip and clip joints, massage parlours and brothels. Very few knew the art galleries, opera house or theatres. Good old Alex took me for a cruise on a junk and I fell in love with the place.

I remembered that cruise years later when the opportunity arose for me to do it again. I eagerly accepted. You see, the magnificently restored old teak cutter that served as the port authority ship in Sydney Harbour for many years was sold to a Hong Kong company. One day, the manager of the company was on board the flight. He invited me to go sailing the following day with his family. It was great sitting in the sun, drinking Tiger beer and eating char-grilled chicken while dodging junks with patched pink sails, ferries, sampans and cargo ships. Pollution had not then invaded the sheltered coves around the back of Victoria Island and it was crystal clear at Sheko Bay — so pure you could see the sandy bottom ten fathoms down.

This was all years ago before tourism took off (and spoiled it). You could spend the whole day wandering around the back streets of the city and not see another tourist. Shopping as we know it today was unheard of — no huge department stores, just little shops and stalls where bartering was expected. It was fun.

Most of the crew took the opportunity to upgrade their uniform shirts here, having them made from fine cotton. The standard issue of heavy cotton shirts given to us by the airline were impossible to keep looking neat. Some even went further and had uniforms made of beautiful wool, but Santa took the cake. He had a pair of pyjamas made just like his uniform, as he claimed the only time he ever had a decent night's sleep was when he was in uniform.

My first three-day stay in Hong Kong passed all too quickly, and when it was time to leave, the crew were down in the foyer of the Ambassador Hotel, 'booted and spurred', waiting for Santa to arrive so we could depart for the airport. Suddenly, the hotel's revolving glass-door clattered around to admit Santa dressed in an electric-blue 'happy coat'. Stencilled across the back in silver lettering was the word 'Ecstasy'. *Hmmm!* He strode quickly across the crowded foyer to the lifts, looking neither left nor right, his skinny, hairy legs sticking out of the bottom of the short coat. We all stood with mouths agape. He never lived it down, and for years insisted he was only in the back-street Ecstasy (everybody knew it doubled as a brothel, patronised mainly by rough-looking merchant seamen) for a sauna. He claimed some 'thieving bastard' had stolen his clothes and he had to borrow the happy coat from one of the girls.

2. Stuck

Who the hell's pressing that bloody call-bell? We were approaching Idlewild Airport, New York, in the middle of a blizzard. The seatbelt sign had been switched on as the plane bumped and bucked all over the sky. As usual, the last-minute race was on, stowing serving trays, teapots and jugs in their respective cupboards. This was all being done one-handed, the other hand holding tightly onto the turbulence grip bolted to the bulkhead.

There it bloody goes again. Glancing quickly over my shoulder at the call light panel, it became clear that the person ringing was not in the cabin, but in the toilet at the rear of the plane. The call bell in the toilets was located thoughtlessly right next to the flush button and everybody seemed to push it repeatedly, mistaking it for the flush. So, it came as no surprise that yet another passenger didn't read the sign or see the red arrow with FLUSH written on it.

Anyway, what the hell is someone doing in the toilet this late? Everybody should be strapped in their seats for landing, I thought to myself.

Weaving my way down to the toilets, I knocked loudly on the door, calling out at the same time, 'Stop ringing that damn bell and hurry up. We are getting close to landing.'

A lady's frightened voice replied from inside. 'Thank goodness you've come. Please help me. I'm stuck.'

Stuck? Stuck? How can she be stuck? She means locked in, surely.

Opening the door from the outside, I was surprised to see a woman of very ample proportions in obvious distress. She was seated on the throne with her frilly pink knickers about her ankles. Instead of sitting on the seat, she had sat directly onto the stainless-steel pan, and the plane, having descended through several thousand feet, had caused a suction. Her very large posterior was drawn down and she was stuck all right, stuck fast.

In a flash I could see the problem and leapt up onto the bench with one foot in the sink, the other across the toilet-roll holder, straddled above her. I reached down and grasped her under the armpits, trying to heave her up. No good. I needed help.

Leaning out of the toilet, I saw Frank, my galley man who had taken over from me, frantically stowing equipment.

'Hey, Frank, quick, give me a hand here,' I shouted.

Frank didn't have the restraint I had. One look at the position I'd taken up over the embarrassed lady caused him to double over and explode into peals of laughter. Then, taking her legs, he also tried to pry her loose.

'This isn't working,' Frank panted. 'Maybe we can twist her off,' he suggested. 'If I get the wooden mixing spoon, I can butter it up and wedge it between her bum and the pan,' he suggested aloud.

'Okay, but first see how close we are to landing,' I gasped.

He came back on the run. 'Leave it Brian, we are over the fence.'

Climbing down from my precarious perch, and with a quick shrug of my shoulders at the wretched lady, we dashed to our seats, clicking on our seatbelts as the plane touched down on the icy runway. The plane's jet engines went into reverse thrust to slow us down. A loud *zoop* came from the toilet. Looking at Frank, who was still laughing, I commented, 'Well, that's either sucked her right in or spat her out.' This caused Frank to become helpless with laughter.

The toilet door at this point was flung open, the poor woman appearing, totally bewildered. The back of her dress was in a hell of a state covered in sticky blue dye from the bowels of the pan. We later saw her being assisted to customs with blue-streaked legs wrapped in an airline blanket. I'll bet she had the shape of that pan on her blue bum for months.

3. Calypso Cola in Cairo

From time to time, notices would appear in the Aircraft Information Book which all crew were supposed to read sometime during the flight. Most of the notices were boring, mundane things, such as not to park our cars in the managers' reserved parking spaces at Mascot, or beware of pickpockets on the Hong Kong ferries, but one notice intrigued me. It read, 'Do not, under any circumstances, accept the local Egyptian Calypso Cola in Cairo. Only accept Coca-Cola or Pepsi-Cola.'

Why? I wondered.

Rum and Cola was the 'in' drink at the time in the Oasis Bar of our hotel in Cairo, but I must admit that with the strong red rum in Egypt, the Calypso Cola (with the haunting face of an ancient Pharaoh on the label) did seem to taste a little strange. Next time I went through Cairo I enquired at the local catering office.

'What's the matter with the Calypso Cola, Mohammed?'

Mohammed's reply made me wish that I hadn't asked. 'The soft drink manager received many, many complaints about the taste of the Cola,' he said, then continued, 'They were very concerned so they decided to shut down production and clean out the huge vats.'

Uh oh, I thought.

Kalah was a tireless, hardworking employee for the soft drink company, but he had one weakness — he could not leave the girls working there alone. Sexual harassment was unheard of then but, had it been recognised, Kalah would have been out the door, hard worker or not, in no time at all.

When they emptied out vat number three, there on the bottom was all that was left of Kalah — his gold teeth, part of his heavy-duty boots, and the silver belt buckle he was so proud of and always wore.

Was he pushed or did he fall?

'Come to the office,' Mohammed said. 'I still have a newspaper clipping of it somewhere.' The clipping was only a paragraph or two on page five of the daily paper, but the last two lines made me burst out laughing. It read: 'It was regrettable that this should happen to Kalah as, according to his brother, he had almost saved enough money for the overseas trip he had always dreamed of having.'

He got it! The only trouble was, he flew on about

twenty different airlines to fifty different countries inside 200,000 bottles of Calypso Cola.

4. Crackers

Mavis Crackenburg — *what a hell of a name.* Mavis also thought so and encouraged everyone to call her Crackers — *and what a hell of a girl she was too.* Crackers had been a flight hostess for eight years now and, before flying, had come from a very successful modelling career (trust the airline to quickly sign her on) and was winner of several beauty contests.

The motto of the crews in the 'good old days' was 'Work Hard, Play Hard', and Mavis — had she been flying then — would have well and truly held her own. Great worker and first down to the crew-room after a flight, bottle of vodka in hand, Crackers was always among the last to leave. She was one of the boys — and could swear like a trooper. Many times, I heard her let slip a four-letter word as we served inflight meals to first-class passengers. The passenger would look at her startled, only to be greeted with a lovely smile. The passenger's expression would change to one of, *No, I must have heard wrong.*

We were flying between Honolulu and Vancouver in Canada one afternoon and Crackers did not seem to be her old self, being irritable and rather sharp with both passengers and crew. We had just finished the lunch service and I was leaning on the bar at the back of the first-class cabin, when Crackers came up and faced me across the bench.

'What's wrong with me, Brian?' she nervously asked, adding, 'I seem to be popular with the boys but nobody wants to go steady with me.'

I'd been waiting for an opportunity to talk to her for some time about this, and I grabbed it with both hands.

'Crackers,' I said, hating what I was about to tell this beautiful-looking girl. 'That's the trouble. You are too much like one of the boys. They think you're great but, with all the swearing and drinking, nobody wants to take you home to meet mother.'

She was visibly hurt by my answer and for the rest of the trip she was very subdued and stayed away from the crew and the crew-rooms. Word filtered back to me some time later that she had left flying and nobody seemed to know what she was doing now. I secretly worried that my harsh answer may have been part of the reason for her leaving.

*

'Good morning, sir,' I said, looking at his boarding pass. 'Straight down this aisle and the crew will seat you … Hello, madam! Go across and down to the right.' The passengers were now crowding the entrance door and I was busy checking boarding cards with just a glance at passengers, when I found myself looking into the smiling eyes of Mavis. She looked radiant. She quickly frowned as I shaped the unspoken word 'Crackers' with my mouth and hurriedly introduced me to her husband. I led the way to the seats 1A and 1B in the first-class cabin, known in the aircraft industry as the VIP seats.

After take-off, she came back to the galley for a chat and, over a cup of tea (like old times), she told me she did indeed smarten up her act after speaking to me that day. She was now happily married to a very prominent member of the High Court, living in a waterfront, harbourside residence with yacht and fancy car. She could have anything she wanted. I wished her well.

She turned to go back to her seat, then turned back again and, with a cheeky smile, said, 'I owe you a f***ing big favour, Brian.' Deep down, Crackers was still here.

5. Pea soup

Good grief! It's back. I had just opened the winter schedule menu for the American run for the sector from San Francisco to Honolulu, prior to handing them out to the passengers. Across the top of the menu, it read, 'Welcome aboard to passengers flying on our airline. We sincerely wish you an enjoyable flight.' It sounded to me like something the Queen's writers would dream up for her to say in one of her speeches to the commoners.

Across the bottom was a one-liner that perturbed most crew, particularly on the American run, and those Yanks with their fat wallets. It simply read: 'Cabin crew are not permitted to accept gratuities. Refusal may offend.' You can bet your bibby it certainly did. One senior steward found a solution to this by spending considerable time cutting the bottom off the menus with a pair of scissors. *Anyway, I can't believe it. There it is:*

American green pea soup
Seasoned salad & Thousand Island dressing
Garlic bread
Beef curry
Apple pie and cream
Tea or coffee
Liqueurs

Bloody hell! Can you imagine what havoc that concoction would brew up in the hardiest of stomachs after the bellyful of cocktails the Yanks usually consumed prior to eating? The first inkling of discomfort appeared like clockwork twenty minutes after the coffee service. Passengers began shifting from one bum cheek to the other with a discreet little fart, but after a further ten minutes the farting had become quite audible here and there in the cabin. Five minutes later it was a crescendo of blatant farting from all those poor souls who had unwittingly partaken of the dreaded, *bloody genuine*, American emerald-green pea, guaranteed-to-make-you-fart soup.

The cabin had by this time taken on an aroma of the North Head Sewerage Treatment Works. Passengers were heading for the toilets down the back in curious crab-like fashion to keep their buttocks together. Meanwhile, the crew were holed up in the galley behind drawn curtains praying the captain would not have to put the seat-belt sign on. Nothing was going to coax us out of the cabin until the pressure eased off.

I like to think I had something to do with the removal of this gourmet item from the winter menu. On this particular day, the soup was loaded as usual in one-gallon metal containers, which fitted into a recess in the galley. When the container was pushed in far enough it connected with an element at the back to keep the soup piping hot.

On take-off out of San Francisco we thundered down the runway, with a strange vibrating metal-to-metal sound coming from within the galley. Sitting strapped in the jump seat I watched in horror as the catch holding the container of green farting liquid worked loose. We roared over the perimeter fence as the container shot out, hitting the opposite wall and flinging off the lid. A sea of steaming green exploded in all directions. *Wouldn't you know it?* The worst affected place was the coat cubicle because the curtain had rattled open during take-off. Neatly labelled passengers' coats were now a dripping mass of green, looking like a St Patrick's Day parade.

What a nightmare of a flight it was from then on! Between feeding the passengers, we were cleaning coats in the galley, which now resembled a Chinese laundry. Frank, my old mate from the-fat-lady-stuck-in-the-toilet incident, was madly dabbing soup from coats, while I held them in front of the open oven, to try and dry them out a bit. Our confidence took a severe plunge when we came to the fox-fur stole. Frank set about removing the soup with the comb from his pocket. Washing the comb under the tap, he asked, 'Well, Brian, you can't say it's not, well, different, flying with you. Are all flights like this?'

'Nearly all,' I had to admit. 'I'm afraid that fur stole you're working on is a lost cause. It has taken on the appearance of a well-groomed dead rat. The owner is going to have a fit when she sees it.'

And she did.

The catch was found to be faulty, letting us off the hook. But it cost the airline plenty in dry-cleaning and replacement charges, accompanied by lots of apologies, bowing and scraping.

Three weeks later I was back in the city-by-the-bay and, once again, I apprehensively opened the menu. Hooray! *'It'* was gone, replaced by a prawn cocktail!

6. Change the Baby

Some passengers have absolutely no sense of humour and everything is a serious business with nothing to laugh at. We learned to read these people as they boarded the aircraft and, even though they got the same good service with a smile, we never became entangled in lengthy conversations. The reason for this was it usually led to doom, gloom and trouble.

I was working with Beverley Brown, who was doing the mandatory patrol around the economy-class cabin one evening after the meal service was finished. An English woman, with a tiny baby, had been down-graded from business-class due to a double booking and was not at all happy. She called Beverley over.

'Yes, madam, can I help?' she beamed brightly.

The English woman thrust her very wet, pale, crying baby into Beverley's arms, demanding with a snarl, 'Change this child immediately!'

Taking the baby down to the rear of the plane, Beverley asked another crew member to mind it for a moment while she went in search of 'something'. She found what she was after in the rear cabin and marched back to the English lady. With a gleam in her eye, Beverley smiled sweetly and held out a beautiful, happy, nut-brown Fijian baby. She asked the stuck-up woman, 'Is this a big enough change, madam?'

Several weeks later, Beverley was called into the office to answer a complaint written by the woman. The boss, who did, thankfully, have a sense of humour, was halfway through giving Bev a dressing-down and asking if she would like a change. Maybe a change of jobs! At this point he could not contain himself any longer and burst out laughing.

7. Have a Nice Day

Can you believe it! I've left my camera on the public transport bus. Standing on the pavement, helplessly watched as the old bus departed, making a hell of a racket and belching out clouds of smoke. On the back of the receding bus was a sign advising tourists that it was 'Courtesy Week' here in Singapore. *Oh well,* I thought, *the rewind was buggered and it didn't take the best of pictures.* I headed down to Alfred's in Dolphin Street, where airline crew was always given a discount. Alfred worked on the principle that, if he looked after us, we would tell passengers on the aircraft about his store, getting him extra business. He was right, as the store was always busy.

Entering the store, air-conditioned to the point where an overcoat would have been comfortable after the heat outside, I was greeted by a pretty young lady in a bright-red cheongsam.

'Hello, sir,' she said with a broad smile. 'Can I get you a cool drink?'

Inside the refrigerated store, the sweat was already congealing on my skin and I was tempted to ask if she had any hot chocolate. She was most helpful, nothing being a bother to her, even though I looked at most of the cameras in stock. As I was on a London trip and would be back here in a week for two days, I decided to buy it then.

'No problem. My name is Jenny. Please ask for me when you come back, and have a safe trip,' the young lady said, smiling brightly.

Back in Singapore from London, around I went looking for Jenny. Flinging the curtain back she came out from the rear of the store, her eyes flashing. 'What you want now?' she snapped at me.

There was no hint of a smile either! *Maybe she has had a bad day*, I thought to myself as I explained, 'I still have not made up my mind on which camera I want.'

'Huh, you Aussies all alike. Not know what you want.'

'Now, wait a moment. What happened to the nice, polite young lady who served me last week?' I enquired.

Her answer still makes me smile, 'Last week "Courtesy Week",' she snapped. 'This week it is "Clean up Singapore".'

8. A Good Day for Flying?

As I walked down to Gate Ten with the crew, even from a distance the old guy standing apart from the other passengers waiting to board puzzled me. Getting closer, I also saw that he had tears in his eyes. Tears in the airport terminal? A common thing, but it struck me that his grieving was, well, somehow different. He was neatly dressed in an out-of-fashion, dark striped suit with wide bell-bottom trousers almost covering his boots. The lapels of his coat were spread out to the width of his shoulders, curling over like two waves about to clash together. Fastened to the left lapel was the old familiar Returned Serviceman's badge. Under the coat was a woollen cardigan, buttoned all the way up, with an untidily knotted black tie peeping out the top. He was nervously rotating the brim of his old, sweat-stained felt hat through his rough farmer-like hands, when his forlorn eyes met mine as I strolled past.

'Is it a good day for flying?' he enquired in a slow, country drawl.

'Yeah mate, fine and clear,' I dryly replied, thinking to myself, *Please don't hold me up, I've got a mile of things to do before receiving passengers.* I hurried on down the ramp to the plane.

The old guy was one of the last to board, holding onto the handrail as he limped down to the aircraft door. Swinging from his shoulder by a strap, pulling his suit even more out of shape, was an ancient airline in-cabin bag. It should have been in an aviation museum, as stencilled on the side in gold were the letters: TEAL. Seeing him, I once again chastised myself for not having given the old man a few moments of my time. Accepting his boarding card, I took him down to his aisle seat, quickly glancing at the passenger next to him. I was relieved to see that she was an elderly lady with a pleasant, homely look about her.

As he sat down, the man said to her, 'Is it a good day for flying?'

'I'll look after you, dear. First time, eh?' she said, patting his hand.

I was helping another passenger nearby with a baby and my heart went out to him as he continued, 'No, it's not the flying that bothers me. You see, me and the missus had our farm foreclosed by the bank and last month she died of a stroke. I reckoned it killed poor old Ethel.' His voice quivered as he added, 'My lifetime swept away in a single month.'

I walked away with tears now brimming in my eyes for the poor old guy who just wanted someone to listen to him. *Next time,* I vowed to myself, *I will.*

9. The Twenty-Pence Bargain

There was a red public telephone box that had a little — well actually, a big — secret among crews. It was situated behind the Mayfair Hotel in London, on the corner of pretty little Green Park. Something was radically wrong with it because if you put a twenty-pence coin in the slot you could dial out to ANYWHERE in the world. For months it was like this, then suddenly it was fixed. Was it because of the queue of three or four people always waiting, with nobody using the one over the road in Bond Street?

10. Len

How Len ever passed the interviews and was accepted as a flight steward was a bit of a mystery to us all. You see, he ... stuttered. It was only on certain words, which he learned to avoid, but there was one word he always had trouble with: cigarettes.

Len and I had been to see a soccer match at Wembley in London and we got off the train at Trafalgar Square in Central London to change to the Circle Line. Len wanted to buy some smokes and headed down to a small kiosk at the end of the platform.

An attractive young lady with beautiful auburn hair, faultless skin, ruby-red lips and smiling blue eyes was serving behind the cluttered counter. Approaching the stall, I casually wondered why such a beautiful girl would choose to work in such a dreary place.

Taking some money from his pocket, Len asked her, 'Do you stock Playfair cig-gi-ci-ci-cigar-cigarettes please?'

'We certainly do,' she replied with a smile, revealing even white teeth. 'Fil-fil-fil-filter or pl-pl-pl-pl-plain, Si-sir?'

Not only did Len stutter but he also had a very short temper to match his curly red hair. Glaring at the girl, and forgetting in his anger the words to avoid, he shouted, 'Sti-sti-stick th-them up you're a-a-a-ar-arse!' Len stormed down the platform. Hurrying along behind, I pondered on why some people wanted to be so cruel.

Several months later, I happened to be in the same station and stopped by the kiosk to buy the local paper. The same young lady was there and, thinking of Len's experience, I turned to walk away when she said, 'Goo-goo-good morning, S-sir, c-can I help you?'

Poor Len, wait until I tell him she stutters worse than he does. Next time he was on a London trip, Len made a detour through Trafalgar Square, stopped and apologised to the young lady for his rudeness.

Eighteen months later they were married in a beautiful little stone village church in the county of Somerset. They now live in Wiltshire, deeply in love, and have three delightful, beautiful, non-stuttering, auburn-haired girls. *How do I know this?* I was best man at their wedding.

11. Calamity

'Brian, your application to be based in London has come through,' my flight controller informed me.

'You little beauty,' I happily replied.

'I have a list of the crew you will be with for the eighteen months you will be flying from there. You'll leave in three weeks' time,' the controller said, handing me the list of names. 'Your skipper will be Captain Shandos,' he concluded with a grin.

Captain Chaos, I thought to myself. *Life will be interesting indeed.*

Most of us opted to live in the county of Surrey, not only because it is so beautiful and mild in winter, but also reasonably close to Heathrow Airport. One of the benefits of the bases was that transport was supplied to and from the airport, the bus doing the rounds of the houses where we lived, picking us up and dropping us back after each trip.

It was a typical dead-of-winter morning as we rounded the corner and slid to a stop on the icy road outside Captain Chaos's home. It was a charming two-storey stone cottage with thatched roof, and an undressed stone chimney, from which swirling grey smoke dissipated in the raw winter air. The window frames and front door were painted in glossy red paint, while contrasting yellow window-boxes, balanced on the window sills, displayed winter flowers. Cherry trees, shrubs and hedges abounded in the garden; a wrought-iron sign hanging at the front gate advised, 'Cherry Tree Cottage'.

His wife (whom everyone called 'Mrs Courageous', because she had to be to marry a man like Chaos) must have picked the house. It was pure English country. Snow was spiralling down, lightly settling on the bare branches of the trees as the weak sun peeped over the bleak hills of Horsell Common.

The bus, with the heater going flat out, was fighting a valiant battle to keep the chilly air at least lukewarm. We huddled, hunched up in our overcoats on the vinyl seats, waiting for Chaos to appear.

By the time Chaos showed up at the front door the snow had increased considerably and even the short run out to the bus had turned him into a snowman. With his usual good cheer and a cheeky grin, he shouted, 'Morning all, lovely day for ducks.' The driver leaned forward, and pressed the starter but the old bus protested — spluttering and coughing. It refused to start, changing Chaos' whole life forever.

Just then, the casement window upstairs opened, the lacy curtains thrust aside, and Mrs Courageous' voice was heard calling sweetly, 'Dear, it's time, my temperature's just gone up!'

With a shrug of the shoulders, Chaos stuck his head out of the bus window and shouted, 'Coming, darling.'

You see, they had been trying for some time to have

a family without success, following all the suggested methods. These included the one-red-sock method, the oysters-and-stout method, and the never-known-to-fail-romantic-on-the-hearth-rug-in-front-of-the-fire method, to no end result. They were now into the Billings way of fertilisation.

Chaos leapt out of the bus grinning to himself, flinging his uniform cap onto the 'Cherry Tree Cottage' sign as he ran quickly past. His tie was draped carelessly on the front door knob just before it slammed shut, followed ten seconds later by the upstairs window and the blind being yanked down.

Still hunched up in the bus, we were busy fantasising on the proceedings going on upstairs. Chaos was back in twenty minutes as if nothing had happened. The whole crew was now waving to Mrs Courageous standing at the window in a next-to-nothing nightie as the bus pulled away. Nine months and two days later, beautiful little Jane was born on the back seat of Chaos' Jaguar halfway to the hospital. Of course, the crew couldn't let a chance like this slip by and nicknamed the little tot 'Calamity'.

12. Sponsored by Coca-Cola

The ship's (aeroplane's) papers in quadruple were handed over to the chief steward by the traffic officer based at each port before departure. Some chiefs just flicked through the bag and accepted that they would be correct, but I was very particular about seeing they were stamped and signed. Without the top copy at least being stamped and signed, entry into the next port of call could be delayed, or even refused, as in a way they were the aircraft's passport.

As we had no traffic officer stationed at either Cairo in Egypt or Karachi in Pakistan, when we flew to these two ports, we had a traffic officer as part of the crew. It was his job to deal with the problems of bookings, seat-allocation, cargo and, of course, the ship's papers.

Up the front of the old 707s, near the galley, there was a small, fold-down desk where the traffic officer filled out forms and made sure everything was in order for arrival at immigration, quarantine and customs.

I was preparing lunch this particular day when I heard Leon, the tall Irish traffic officer, whom everybody called Lofty, exclaim, 'Oh no! Sh*# Sh*# Sh*#!' His huge fist smashed down on the desk top, sending papers, ink pad, coffee cup and staples in all directions as he sat staring bug-eyed at the ship's papers. They were not stamped or signed!

Had the Olympics included drinking in the games, Lofty would have been a certain bet to represent Australia, but seeing how unlikely that was, he would have to be content to be a legend in the airline. Lofty sat there with his head in his hands, trying to get up the courage to go up to the flight deck and tell the captain the glad tidings. They may have to return to Cairo.

'You may be able to forge it,' I suggested. A glimmer of hope appeared on his face. 'If we boil up a champagne cork,' I continued, 'it will make the thing swell to about double the size. You may be able to make your own stamp as they did in prisoner-of-war camps during World War II.'

'If it doesn't work, it's going to be World War III up there,' Leon said, indicating the flight deck with his thumb.

The cork, after boiling in the jug, swelled up as predicted and Leon, taking the razor blade out of his kit, began carving the spread-eagle insignia of Egypt on the cork, copied from an Egyptian coin. It turned out to be surprisingly quite good, so he stamped each copy with his ink pad, smudging them a little to disguise the irregularities. The flight was by this time past the point of no return, so he was committed. Do or die, or, as the IRA motto goes, 'Once in, never out'. Maybe 'Do or be Sacked' was more appropriate.

'Now for the tricky part,' said Lofty, who was warming to the whole thing. He was busy looking for some form of running writing in Arabic as a signature when he spied the box of Coca-Cola bottles stacked in the galley by the Egyptian caterers. They were labelled in Arabic. After having about a dozen practice runs of copying

'Coca-Cola' in the Arabic lettering to get it right, Leon confidently signed under the spread-eagle stamp.

On arrival in Karachi, it was a very nervous, hungover Irish traffic officer who walked across the tarmac to the terminal.

'Brian, if I get away with this, I'm going to give up the drink for a month,' Leon said.

'Let's not go overboard,' I replied to this outrageous remark.

The quarantine and immigration officers hardly looked at the stamped copies, passing the crew on to customs. Leon was back to his old self and confidently presented the forms to the customs officer who looked more closely at them but also didn't see anything wrong. We were all waved through.

Leon and I never told the captain what had been done but, *boy oh boy*, what a party we had that night. Rum and Cokes of course, and Leon was in top form already, having forgotten his promise of that morning, singing an old Andrews Sisters' hit of the 1940s and drinking Rum and Coca-Cola.

13. Mr Smooth

If the aircraft had been on schedule, the crew would probably not have had the pleasure of meeting Mr

Smooth. We were sitting in the old terminal of Hong Kong International Airport at Gate 22, waiting for the arrival of the plane. Most of the crew were gazing into space, thinking of home, barbecues, sleeping in or holidays, the latter being a favourite gazing pastime.

Mr Smooth came strutting down to where we were sitting, dressed in his new striped tailor-made suit, Ivy League-monogrammed shirt, hand-made white shoes and Panama hat. If he was trying to achieve the Mr Wheeler Dealer look, he had certainly done so.

As he approached Gate 22, he whipped out a digital telephone. I should explain this incident occurred at the time when digital phones were a novelty and a big status symbol. Not like now when it's similar to bums — everybody has one. Anyway, Mr Smooth pretended to dial a few numbers, glancing our way to make sure he had our attention, then proceeded to give the person who answered a hard time. It went like this: 'Hank, sell 50,000 High-Ten gold mine shares TODAY. I don't want any excuses, you hear. To hell with the snow in New York. Get down to the Stock Exchange NOW and SELL.'

The business deal was being shouted in a broad Australian accent, so loud they must have been able to hear him down at Gate 17. Yes, he had our attention.

'Listen carefully, Hank. Get your arse down there quick smart and, while you're at it, buy 80,000 Frankston Steel shares. Remember, your job's on the line if you don't get them,' he growled into the telephone.

By this time, we had all sat up, listening intently to this high roller business conversation, the hosties eyeing him up and down with renewed interest as well.

'Hank,' he continued, 'don't let me down.' Then his phone rang!

14. The lottery

Each time the plane landed at a transit stop on the way to its destination, the flight engineer deplaned to supervise the refueling and any maintenance needing attention. He also strolled around underneath, checking the flaps, ailerons and the aircraft skin for damage by birds sometimes hit in flight.

His last 'little' job was to divide the nose wheel into twelve segments on the side wall of the tyre with chalk, numbered like a clock. On the old Boeing 707s there were twelve crew and everybody in the crew was expected to put in a dollar, then draw out a number from one to twelve from a crew hat. On landing at the next port of call, and after the chocks had been put in place, whoever had the number nearest the ground won the twelve bucks. It was a decent-sized pot in the 1960s. Then the inevitable happened.

An executive of the airline standing in the departure lounge saw the nose wheel and reported it. Yet another order in our files, this time about defacing company property. Action, demotion, the sack — *yeah, yeah, we had heard it all before.* It did kill our fun, though.

As a result, we decided to do 'the lottery' another way. A guessing game was introduced for the length of time it took the crew bus from start-up at the airport to stopping outside the hotel. We would spend the trip looking at our watches, telling the driver (who took no notice) to speed up or slow down, hampered or helped by red and green traffic lights, traffic snarls, slow pedestrians on crossings and peak-hour traffic. This was even more fun.

15. Ricky

Ricky was a terror for the drink. It didn't really matter if it was bourbon, scotch, vodka or gin strained through an Afghan camel driver's jock strap, it all went down the hatch nicely, thank you very much.

The trouble started when he began 'sipping' on the flights. We all knew it was taboo, and an aviation law that partaking of the amber fluid within eight hours of flying was punishable by disciplinary action, demotion or the sack. I think Ricky in his stewed state got it mixed up and thought the rule was 'eight feet from landing'.

Tony, the flight service director, signed on in Sydney

for the fifteen-day trip to London, casually running his eye down the crew list. He stopped short. Sweat broke out on his brow and, groaning aloud, he said, 'Oh no, not Ricky. Please, anybody but Ricky.'

Everybody knew about Ricky's problem but no one wanted to put the finger on him. It was typical of crews years ago who covered for a workmate. The funny thing was, when he was sober or temporarily off the booze, he did a first-rate job. He gave passengers fine service and was liked by all, but when he hit the bottle, he became a bloody menace.

Turning to me with an exasperated look on his face, Tony lamented, 'What am I going to do? I could handle a few days, but fifteen? Heaven help us.'

'Read the riot act to him, Tony,' I answered, knowing deep down it wouldn't help if Ricky went on a binge.

'Right,' Tony growled, lighting up a cigarette to calm his nerves. 'If I've got to fly with him, it's going to on my terms.'

We waited by the tea and coffee vending machine for inoffensive-looking Ricky to sign on.

'Righto, Ricky,' Tony said, pouncing on him. 'Let's get it straight from the start. NO drinking on board. I mean it and, if you do, you will leave me no choice but to send you home.'

Ricky, totally at ease, casually leaning against the coffee vending machine (he had heard this lecture before), looked Tony in the eye. 'Take it easy, Tony,' he said in his disarming way. 'You'll end up having a seizure and, anyway I've given up the filthy habit. You haven't got a worry in the world.'

Not entirely believing this statement, Tony kept a close eye on him for the first sector up to Singapore and could not fault his service to the passengers.

Maybe I have been a bit harsh on the poor bugger in not believing him, Tony thought to himself. Singapore to Bahrain was a similar performance and Tony began to relax and look forward to his stay in London.

Just prior to serving breakfast two hours out of London, Tony watched Ricky set up the 'good morning juices' on a silver tray. Was that a stagger? No, he's off the booze, Tony thought, going back to his paperwork. His first and biggest mistake.

By the time we flew over the White Cliffs of Dover at 20,000 feet, Ricky was still at 40,000, totally legless. He was put into the crew-rest with the curtains drawn as the captain, technical crew and passengers disembarked, while from behind the curtains the strains of 'Danny Boy' slurred forth. After the last passenger departed, the problem now was how to get Ricky down to the customs hall and into the crew bus.

Tony waited half-an-hour before making his move, figuring the technical crew and passengers should have all cleared formalities by then and were heading for town. 'After all,' he said, 'there's no need to cause a commotion, is there?' He had joined the long list of coverers.

The senior customs man, leaning his knuckles on the desk, asked Tony, 'Anything to declare? Liquor? Cigarettes?' Tony, who had put Ricky on a bag trolley and looking down at slumbering Ricky, with far more duty-free booze inside him than was allowed for the entire crew, with a jerk of the thumb replied, 'Only the chief steward.' Without the slightest hint of a change in his expression, the customs man replied, 'Straight on through, thank you.'

16. Give Them Nothing

Years ago, there was a notoriously cranky old chief steward whom nobody liked to fly with. No matter what you asked of him on the aircraft, he would snarl at you, 'Give them nothing.' This was surely a dangerous practice.

The inevitable day arrived when he had as his galley man a new recruit fresh out of the airport school. The happy-go-lucky Fijian caterers at Nandi, Fiji's airport, were busy loading the first-class supper and breakfast food to be served on the next sector to Honolulu.

'What do you think of these lobsters, Chief?' the new recruit asked, peeling back the foil covering. Looking up irritably from reading the sports page of the newspaper in the crew-rest, the chief steward said out of the corner of his mouth, 'Give them nothing,' then went back to his reading.

Gee, this fellow's good to fly with, the new man happily thought, off-loading all the food for that sector to the amazement of the catering staff.

They took off for Honolulu and a short time into the flight the chief growled at the galley man, 'Have the supper ready in twenty minutes and we start breakfast one hour sharp before arrival.'

The new man gasped, then told him what he had done.

'What? You did WHAT?' the chief said, open-mouthed and stunned.

In a panic, he had to pretty-up Business meals for the first-class passengers who were not very impressed with the cuisine. Meanwhile, back in Fiji, the Fijians in catering were having a wonderful time.

You guessed it! The chief NEVER used his standard answer again, and all the stewards he had bawled out over the years revelled in him finally getting his just desserts.

17. Magic Word

Whatever happened to the magic word 'please'? I was beginning to wonder. It was one of those flights where you just wanted it to end, get off, have a couple of beers and forget it. The majority of passengers were ill-mannered and just plain awful.

I know that's one of the things we are trained for, immune to, and also paid to accept, but now and then it gets to you — particularly if it is practically a whole plane full of them.

They were Americans from New York City working for a huge transport company. As a bonus to their employees, the company had bought a package deal for them to spend a weekend in San Francisco.

'Gimme a coffee.'

'Hey, buddy — Coke.'

'You, where's my Martini? And hold the ice.'

'Two beers here and make it snappy.'

'What's for dinner?' someone asked, pulling on the back of my coat. It went on like this for two hours, until the crack finally appeared in my armour and I blurted out in a loud voice, 'Doesn't anybody know the magic word?'

The very next person I served was a reserved-looking, middle-aged lady, probably a secretary, who timidly asked, 'Could I have a f***ing scotch and water?'

Wrong magic word. And still no sign of a 'please'.

18. Hong Kong

When I began flying sixty years ago, Hong Kong was the most fascinating place in the world that we went to, staying there for three days before moving on. The streets were cobbled, dimly lit at night and dominated by rumbling red rickshaws, particularly in the narrow, winding back streets. They were not only used to convey passengers, but also as light trucks delivering goods to the 'nation of shopkeepers', piled high and pulled by skinny Chinese men.

Many of the old buildings were constructed in the colonial colonnade style, standing shoulder to shoulder with go-downs (warehouses). Tranquil, pastel shades were used to paint the buildings with contrasting coloured shutters to keep out the noonday heat, dust and noise. Old, wispy-bearded men with rheumy eyes and gazes of a thousand metres sat in doorways, sucking on smoky, bamboo opium pipes, dreaming of the past.

Scaffolding on construction sites was all made of flexible bamboo poles going up the outside of buildings — ten or more stories — like an out-of-control vine. The scaffolders wore a curious two-toed rubber boot for climbing, tying the joints with strips of cane hanging from their waistbands. The labouring work was mainly done by women decked out in dark, neck-to-ankle clothing with a fringed, conical rattan hat pulled low down on their heads. They fetched sand, cement and bricks in baskets shouldered on the ends of long bamboo poles, jogging along in time to the bouncing baskets.

A well-known European scaffolding company saw a big chance to break into the market and make a killing, and succeeded in winning the contract for a couple of hotels under construction. Everything went well until the first winds heralded a cyclone and gale-force winds. Within hours the steel tubing erected fifteen storeys high began to twist, bend outwards and collapse in a heap on the street. There must have been a lot of 'I-told-you-so' and nodding of heads from the bamboo riggers whose scaffolding swayed and creaked but remained intact.

Machinery such as bulldozers, cranes, jackhammers, cement mixers and the like were not used as it would have spelled doom to millions of labouring jobs. Indeed, to prove the point, the area around Kai Tak Airport is extremely mountainous and, as tourism took hold, bigger planes were being built, requiring longer runways. The existing runway had a mountain at the end of it. To lengthen it, the mountain was simply ... removed. It was dumped into the harbour all by hand using pick, shovel and wheelbarrow, doubling the old runway's length.

Meals-on-wheels were everywhere. Light carts with large-spoked wheels equipped with steaming urns and woks served noodles, rice and many unrecognisable dishes. They did a fast trade with the locals but tourists were strongly advised against eating at them because of the lack of hygiene. The bubbling food itself was probably all right but the method of washing the cracked, chipped bowls over the open drains behind the stalls, was enough to turn off the hardiest of tourists. To eradicate the rat problem the simple but effective method was, when a rat was caught, to pop it into a tin bolted on the telegraph poles throughout the city. These tins were called rat bins and, looking inside one, I often wondered what the sizzling liquid was that dissolved the rodents.

Little taverns dotted the side streets before the big, new hotels were built — places like 'Ned Kelly's', 'Matilda's' and 'Joe's & Jim's Joint', where the music coming from within was either soft and suggestive or rock-and-roll, with waitresses strutting about in scanty clothing, their wooden-soled shoes click-clacking on the stone floors. A lot of taverns doubled as houses of ill-repute; smelling strongly of stale beer and sin. The main patrons were tough-looking, roughly dressed, tattooed merchant seamen from the cargo boats.

There were peddlers selling everything imaginable, shoe menders, pick-pockets, beggars, touts for tailor shops, and small boys strategically positioned near muddy puddles who would spit-polish your shoes for ten cents. Umbrella sellers did a roaring trade in the monsoon season selling roughly made bamboo brollies covered in fish skin. They only cost a few cents to buy and, when you got to where you were going, you simply tossed it on the pavement where it was snatched up to be resold again and again.

Just west of the Kowloon ferry building, the old Queen Elizabeth was permanently anchored in mid-harbour being used as a university and hotel. One night it sank under mysterious circumstances, settling on the bottom, listing to port, the superstructure and funnels visible above the waterline. It lay for a long time like this as a continuous stream of rust-coloured water wended its way down the harbour. Eventually she was unceremoniously broken up for scrap.

The insidious destruction of old Hong Kong has spread uptown like a plague as far as Mong Kok. This area is the last bastion and, if you ignore the McDonald's and other fast-food stores, you can still believe you are in timeless China, complete with the things mentioned earlier that have disappeared from downtown. The old Hong Kong I knew has been obliterated — the character, charm and excitement coming down with the dust of the old buildings.

Ah, yes, I often sigh. The mystique and intrigue have all but gone now.

Progress has shot itself nicely in the foot, yet again.

19. Passenger Comments

I once asked a Canadian on the aircraft what she most liked during her stay in Australia. Her reply was stunning, 'I just loved those kangaroo bears.' I asked the same question of an Indian from Bombay, who said in a sing-song voice how amazed he was at so many parked cars in Sydney. A woman thought for a moment, then said what a mammoth feat it was that we had constructed a sandstone seawall all the way around Sydney Harbour. I'd never noticed.

'Being able to have an early morning stroll around Centennial Park totally alone,' Mr Kinoshita from Japan said. 'An impossible feat, day or night in crowded Tokyo.'

'Unwrapped sweets, how unhygienic,' the stuck-up English woman replied in her hoity-toity voice. I was tempted to say, 'Dogs in the butcher shops was okay, though?'

Americans know very little about our country, I discovered. Many times, I was asked to say something in my native tongue.

The Korean man said he was amazed to see adult male tourists in shorts. In Korea men never wear shorts after their fourteenth birthday.

'Your wines are not any good,' the Frenchman said.

'Oh, really?'

The German's answer was also short: Our rules and regulations are about as good as theirs.

'To be sure, it's a grand place,' the softly spoken Irishman said.

20. Shiners

In the 1960s you had to be on guard all the time for practical jokes perpetrated by fellow crew members, but at times I thought they went a bit too far. To get a fix on their present position, the flight navigator of the old 707, would push up a periscope through the roof of the cockpit and peer around at the stars — yes, he actually did. Anyway, our hostesses were this insensitive navigator's targets and, like me, they were fascinated and dying to have a look. What he would do was wait until the hostess was about to help serve the first-class passengers' breakfast. He would then invite the poor girl up for a quick look, and tell her to screw her eye into the rubber for a good seal. What he didn't tell her was that he had rubbed carbon paper around the rubber eye piece. It gave the most magnificent black eye appearance and, as the breakfast service was already underway, she would rush out through the curtain, astounding passengers with her appearance. A chief once told me he could not look at the poor girl for fear of laughing as she not only had one black eye, but two, as she had changed eyes and now looked like a racoon.

21. Auckland PAs

I used to crack up listening to PA (public address) announcements at Auckland International Airport, 'Would all pissengers on Flight Sex please chick at Chickin Desk Tin for departure times and upgrade lust.'

22. Dobbers

On a flight very early in my flying career, Norm — an old-hand chief steward of many years — huffing and puffing on a roll-your-own cigarette, advised me, 'Never fall out with the crew. You don't always have to fit in with what they want to do, but never get on the outer with them either.'

This was sound advice I was to follow for the next thirty years as I saw many retaliations done to those who did the wrong thing, or committed the mortal sin of dobbing someone in to Management. Our superiors back in the office encouraged this tittle-tat among the weaker crew members, but thankfully most abided by the motto, 'We fix our own problems'.

More than once I saw a crew member open his briefcase for inspection in customs after a long flight to find a melting ice-cream cake or chocolate gateau inside. Ringing someone up in the middle of the night and telling him it was call time for a flight was a mean trick, I always thought. Nevertheless, it went on, and there would be the poor bugger 'booted and spurred' ready down in the foyer of the hotel with the receptionist insisting, 'But sir, it's only 1:30 am.' Worst of all were those who were not invited to crew drinks or a party. There were and always will be the 'double debriefers' as they were called, who after debriefing with the crew would stay back on some pretext and blow the whistle.

Ah, yes Norm, I often thought. Thanks for that sound advice.

23. Babylon

Across the Nile from the southern tip of Rhoda Island in the middle of Cairo is the old quarter, known as Babylon. It survives today eight metres below street level thanks to Trajan, the Roman Emperor, who had built a stone defence wall completely surrounding it before the birth of Christ.

Incidentally, the Holy Family sheltered here on their flight into Egypt from the clutches of King Herod. At that time, the pyramids were already 2,000 years old. A church had been built over the spot in ancient times with a stone stairway leading down under the church to the place where bullrushes grow, which is where Moses was found in a basket by the Pharaoh's daughter and became part of the royal family.

Babylon is entered by descending a set of steps similar to entering a modern subway. In twenty seconds, you go back thousands of years. You could walk past this set of steps day after day for years without realising what you were missing. It is a complete contrast to the chaotic mayhem and noisy traffic above — here, only the occasional donkey and cart are seen wending their way along cobbled streets. Flanked on both sides of these narrow lanes are crumbling mud and straw houses, unchanged for centuries.

24. Little Nancy

Little Nancy was about two years old, travelling with her parents in business class. She was so pretty and happy, sitting with a little hat perched on her head. Crew passing by could not resist stopping to speak to her or to give her an affectionate little tickle.

When it was time to serve the business-class meal, I offered to take Nancy while her parents had their dinner. After a while, Maureen, who was working with me wanted to carry her — then Sue — then Angela — then, well she didn't mind at all who carried her around.

The galley phone rang from the flight deck requesting cups of tea. When I took the tea up to them, the captain was sitting in the crew-rest having a break and reading the newspaper. As I gave him his cup, he lowered the paper and there, in the crook of his arm was placid little Nancy, fast asleep. We all missed our kids when we were away. Kids like Nancy helped us to cope.

25. The one-shoe shuffle

Captain Ross was great to fly with, but he is gone now. When you flew with him in command, like Santa, you could expect funny things to happen. We made it to Karachi in Pakistan before the 'incident' occurred. Can you believe it? He actually lost one of his shoes during the flight. We searched high and low for it without success.

How could you lose a shoe? Only Captain Ross could! So, what did he do? Simple. He ordered the whole crew to only wear one shoe through the customs hall and out to the crew bus parked in the street — this also included the hostess who was wearing medium-high heels, limping along behind.

I laugh every time I think about it.

26. Two Little Words

The captains were a mixed lot. The majority were great to fly with, but one or two of the old World War II guys still thought they were above everyone else, treating cabin crew with disdain. One such pilot had everybody, including technical crew, jumpy. He was very arrogant and he treated everybody pretty roughly — very much the commander and quick to jump on tiny mistakes — no fun at all.

The galley phone rang and an anonymous steward answered it. 'Four teas now, flight deck,' the captain said.

'Get fucked,' the steward replied and hung up.

The captain was out of the cockpit in moments to find no one in the galley, cabin crew all being busy in the cabin. Wisely, nobody owned up. Surprising how two words could change a person's attitude. It only took a day or two in crew-rooms around the world for everybody, including the technical crew, to be laughing at him.

It didn't help his image. He changed overnight. I was one of those who evacuated the galley that day, and can't tell you who it was as he is still flying.

27. Here It Is

When I ventured out onto the streets wherever I was, I dressed like the locals. No you-beaut Gucci shirts, designer jeans, dangling gold chain around my neck, fancy wristwatch, wallet in the back pocket, and definitely no bum bag buckled around the waist advertising to all the thieves within a mile: Here it is, my money, credit cards, traveller's cheques and passport — come and get it!

28. Silhouette

The second officer really fancied himself as a ladies' man and was always bragging about his 'experiences'. We didn't believe him.

In the middle of the compound at Speedbird House in Karachi, Pakistan, was an old trestle about twenty feet (three metres) high that once supported a water tank. The trestle was still there but the tank was long gone. It was twilight as we sat under the pergola covered in flowering red bougainvillea for an evening drink. There were quite a few from our flights, plus a sprinkling of Lufthansa and KLM crew.

The full moon was rising behind the old trestle this balmy night, when our bragging officer appeared on the platform, then helped one of the hosties up also.

We were given no doubt of his ability, as in silhouette, with the huge bright moon as a backdrop, he made love to the hostess, oblivious that he had an audience. Nobody called out. We were all spellbound, and then crept away to think of home, wives, sweethearts and family. As I left, all the bearers (servants) were peering over the hedge.

29. Drop the Bridgestones

The long night flight from steamy Karachi in Pakistan was nearly over, the wheels being lowered for the approach and landing into Tehran Airport, Iran, covered in a thick blanket of snow. The captain, hearing the grinding sound of the mechanism in operation, turned to me sitting behind him, saying, 'That sound always reminds me of when I was doing a command training check to become a captain into this very port years ago.'

With a wry grin, he continued, 'I hadn't made any mistakes during the whole flight with the check captain listening and watching every move I made until it was time to lower the wheels. My confidence was swelling. I knew I had passed. I was tired and, in a lapse of concentration, shouted to the co-pilot, "Drop the Bridgestones".' He shook his head, reliving the moment and how the co-pilot was looking at him open-mouthed with a shocked expression on his face.

I knew I'd blown it. The check captain, with clenched teeth, failed me on the spot. 'The undercarriage, mister, the undercarriage,' he boomed.

Even today when I see a Bridgestone advertisement on TV, I cringe at the memory of that flight. I had to wait another year before I got the four gold bars on my shoulder, not to mention the pay that went with it.

30. What Do You Do for a Crust?

'What do you do for a crust?' the person asked at a party.

'I'm a flight steward,' I answered.

Immediately, she or he would Oh! and Ah! at the idea of zipping around the world having fun, and of course, the glamour of it all.

Glamour? The real reason cabin crew were originally employed by airlines was for the safety and wellbeing of passengers — it still is. Fires, heart attacks, sickness, crashes, hijacks and violent passengers are all covered each year with a refresher course. Serving drinks and caviar were added later.

Turbulence is the cause of a surprising number of injuries, particularly the clear-air form, simply because the passengers choose to ignore the captain and crew who continually warn them to buckle up. To be flattened on the ceiling then flung onto the floor or armrest of a seat is no joke, I can tell you.

Group tours and football teams have occasionally been a threat to crew in the past if they ganged together and defied our order to behave. A few years ago, there was an incident where a bunch of footballers, when told to behave themselves, beat up the stewards, stripped the hostess down to her underwear and became very ugly to anyone who went near them. The flight engineer saved the day. Putting on a full-face oxygen mask and fire-fighting gloves, he unclipped a CO2 fire extinguisher and went down, firing the white foam at them. That, combined with the extinguisher's noise, caused the footballers to go to water and settle down, not knowing the captain had radioed ahead for the police to meet the aircraft on arrival. They didn't know that there was a possible jail term in store for them.

31. Bouncy Bits

Bahrain in the Arabian Gulf has one of the most exclusive clubs on earth called the Awali Club. It is about eight miles out of the city, completely isolated with not a single thing in sight except sand dunes and more sand dunes. Like most things in oil-rich Arabia, it is over-the-top-magnificent, with flowering gardens, fountains everywhere, pool, tennis courts, bars, billiard room — the works. It would have been at home on 'the strip' in Las Vegas. The club is surrounded by a huge stone wall, topped with broken glass, and it had the most elaborate wrought-iron entrance gates.

Airline crew, for reasons I could never fathom, were welcome to go out to this exclusive club, show their airline ID card and spend the day in luxury. Harry, the chief steward, declared he was going out there for the day and I decided to join him to experience this lavishness. The taxi dropped us off out the front — we showed our IDs and we were in. I headed down to the bar for a drink. Harry said he was going for a swim.

I was only there about fifteen minutes, sipping my drink in the extravagant surroundings, then wandering into the billiard room. Wham! This was championship material. It was unbelievable. Speaking to the pool room manager, I was told that when the table was delivered, a spare slate top came with it and the best way to keep it was to bury it in sand — plenty of that was about. They duly buried it outside and now couldn't find it!

At this point my name was called over the PA to report to reception IMMEDIATELY. What now? Is the airline trying to contact me for a flight?

I could see straightaway that the manager was annoyed, waiting in the foyer, hands on hips and looking like thunder. Uh oh. This was serious. He told me to collect the chief steward from the pool area and to leave without delay. Puzzled, I walked out to the sparkling Olympic-sized pool and stopped dead.

In a country where bare skin is frowned upon, there on the diving board was Harry — stark naked, bouncing up and down while parts of his anatomy were also bouncing about. The women working there had never seen anything like this spectacle and stood spellbound, looking through their spread fingers.

We were escorted down through the manicured

gardens by security guards and out through the gates, which slammed shut behind us. Great. Evicted from the most exclusive club on earth and told not to come back. Harry told me lamely he had forgotten his swimmers and didn't think the Arabs would mind! We were lucky not to be arrested. But how were we going to get back to town?

The gates opened and a white Cadillac glided out and stopped next to us. The tinted window slid down and an American simply said, 'Get in, guys.' He told us between bursts of laughter that it was the funniest thing he had ever seen.

32. Uncommon Sense

When you think that there were three intensive interviews to negotiate, plus a government security check, then a medical examination and three to four months in the 'college of knowledge' under close scrutiny to become a hostess or steward, it makes you wonder how some of these crew members slipped through the net — the absurd things they did with little common sense. But then, a prime minister once quoted Voltaire and remarked that, 'Common sense is not so common'.

33. The Motorbike Affair

As I've said, most of our captains were beaut guys and good fun to fly with — but there was one chap who was ex-World War II RAAF who could be a pain even though as a war hero, he had our respect. He called cabin crew 'cabin staff' which galled us very, very much. Like it or not, we were crew!

It was my fortune to be flying with this captain to Japan one sunny afternoon, and delivering cups of tea to the flight deck. The captain turned round to me and demanded to know in a condescending voice if there were any interesting people on board.

Why I said to him what I said to him has puzzled me ever since. Guess it was his attitude towards me.

'We have Mr H, the manufacturer of bikes and cars, seated in 1A (VIP seat) and he has just given me, for excellent service, a motorbike,' I replied.

Before I could say it was a joke, he leapt out of his seat, heading for the first-class cabin. Blundering through the curtain and welcoming Mr H on board with a big cheesy smile (a bit late), he added, 'If there is anything I or the cabin staff could do, just ask.' He was receiving very blank looks from Mr H who did not speak English very well. Giving up, he flung back the curtain and said to me, standing in the galley, 'I'm the commander of the aircraft and that motorcycle should be mine. After all, you are only a steward.'

That settled it! A lowly steward, hey? Well, I am not going to come clean now. The rest of the flight was very tense indeed.

On the crew bus heading for the hotel, he had another go at me, demanding to know the model of the imaginary motorbike, and had I reconsidered his opinion on who should own it. I was ready for this and said, 'It would be a serious loss of face to hand over the motorbike and it might cause an international incident for the airline if Mr H was to find out.' End of story. I flew with him several times later on — he ignored me and still called us 'staff'.

34. Don't Feed the Convicts

In the good old days, when flying was fun, Calcutta in India was a shipping port of two days for crew. But before disembarking from the aircraft we had a little job to do.

The grass right up to the edge of the runways and across to the aircraft parking at the terminal was all cut by hand. There were ten men doing this work, wielding what looked like sickles with broom handles attached.

Yes, they were convicts from the prison who had volunteered to do this work. Who wouldn't want to get out for the day? They were not dangerous prisoners but 'in' for minor crimes.

The warder guarding these guys was a huge man dressed in a shabby uniform that was once a blue colour. He was always sprawled back in a fold-up chair under a large umbrella pushed into the ground, with BOAC stencilled around the edge. His .303 rifle, in a dreadful state of repair, was carelessly dropped beside him in the grass. I doubt it could be fired or if indeed it was even loaded.

It became the thing to give the guard a couple of packs of cards, a pen or two, and first pick of the dainty tray of sandwiches left over from first-class. He would then let us give the rest to these poor chaps who grabbed handfuls and even put some into their filthy pockets for later.

This went on for months until the office back in Sydney heard about it and the inevitable order was put in our files. Don't feed the convicts. We ignored it. A second warning was issued, stating disciplinary action would be taken against those who chose to ignore the order. It was good while it lasted but I would have liked to have met the heartless person who gave the order. Funny how they were always cutting the grass on Tuesday and Friday afternoon next to Gate 6 where we usually parked — Hmm.

35. Don't Feed the Dogs

When one door shuts, another one opens. We usually flew into New Delhi on a Wednesday and Friday in transit. New Delhi had a huge problem with mangy dogs roaming around the airport. If they had bothered to fix the holes in the chain-wire fence around the perimeter it would have solved the problem. But no, they chose to try catching them, and then new ones would appear. Yes, we started feeding the dogs with left-over smoked salmon, chicken and ham sandwiches.

The station manager once told me how funny it was to see a pack of yapping and barking dogs of all sizes, who recognised our aircraft and merrily trotted along behind as we taxied in. Don't feed the dogs, came the order. I asked the traffic office if the order came from management here at New Delhi and he said it had. In a country where many people didn't have enough to eat, here we were in full view of a crowded airport giving food to stray dogs. How lucky we are in Australia, as that had not occurred to us.

36. Vera

Sitting in the very front seat of the aircraft was Vera Lynn, the famous World War II-era singer. She sang songs that roused the population during a time of crisis.

Vera asked me if I was a singer with my deep voice. 'Yes,' I replied. 'I once sang in a small choir before Pope John Paul in the Basilica in Rome.' She was a charming and easy-going person and I suggested maybe we could sing a song here in the aisle. 'Why not?' was her reply.

There'll be blue birds over the white cliffs of Dover. What a thrill that was for me!

37. Pickles

In the crew-room, Dennis was telling me he had just acquired a 'sniffer' dog that was being retired from the quarantine department at Kingsford Smith International Airport.

'What kind of dog is it, Den?' I asked.

'It's a beagle,' he replied, adding, 'Did you know they are the best sniffers for looking for fruit? His name is Pickles. When I did the shopping for groceries and returned home the first time after getting him, I put the bags on the kitchen bench and Pickles barked and barked, trying to climb onto the bench. I realised he wanted to do his little job.' Dennis continued, 'So now I have to line up all the bags on the kitchen floor, for him to find and point at the fruit and then get his reward.'

38. My Dad

I was looking out the kitchen window at home one afternoon watching my six-year-old son, Bart, playing with two other six-year-old boys from down the street. I heard one of them say, 'My dad's a fireman.' Then the other boy piped up, saying, 'My dad's a policeman.'

They both looked at Bart when he proudly said, 'My daddy's Qantas.' God bless him.

39. The Camper

Everything was serene. All the first-class passengers were fast asleep as I tip-toed around doing the night patrol in the dark cabin. I promptly fell over something in the middle of the cabin. Cursing, I picked myself up while a passenger, decked out in striped pyjamas, was doing the same thing.

I couldn't believe it — he had set up a camp stretcher in the aisle in the cabin! His explanation was that he had a very important boardroom meeting the next day and wanted to be fresh for it. The commotion had woken up all the other passengers as he calmly got back into the makeshift bed.

'This is ridiculous. It's against company safety regulations. You will have to return to your seat,' I said.

'Go away and leave me alone,' he growled.

'It's against company regulations,' I insisted.

'Oh, yeah?' he replied. 'What are you going to do about it?' he asked as he settled himself back into the camp stretcher.

He left me no option. My old mate, Frank, shaking his head, helped me lift up the end, tipping him out onto the carpet.

Yet another disgruntled customer, I happily thought, as I folded up the bed.

40. Dennis and the Love Letter

Dennis was a square peg in a round hole — and there were plenty more in the airline business. Dennis was also a bit naïve.

We were on a trip to Singapore and Dennis kept talking about a girl down in Economy going to Singapore on a shopping holiday.

'Yeah, yeah, Dennis. Have you served the coffee yet?' I asked.

I was surprised when walking into the crew-room at the hotel to find Dennis all dressed up and talking to the girl from the flight whom he had invited for a date.

On the trip home, leaving her in Singapore, he was in love! Dennis was in the galley trying to write a letter to her and not getting very far — he asked me for my help. I wrote out a paragraph of girlie love. The hostie came in to get a coffee, read my attempt and asked for the pen, writing a paragraph of Barbara-Cartland-style love. The second officer said he would like to add a bit. It went from oozing love to quite raunchy! Later in the flight, there was Dennis meticulously copying out the love letter. I asked him if he was actually going to send it.

I didn't see Dennis for over a year. Then, as I was walking through the Bangkok markets, there was Dennis buying baby clothes. He told me it had been a whirlwind courtship; they had married six months later and were expecting their first child. He smiled at me and said, 'It was the letter that did the trick!'

I still wonder if he was pulling my leg. Guess I'll never know.

41. Rudi

The Jewish gentleman was not at all well. He was lying stretched flat out on his back on the carpet in the aisle of C-zone not breathing and with no hint of a heartbeat. Meanwhile, the latest James Bond movie being screened continued on its merry way.

Rudi, a big, rough-and-ready, likeable steward who had migrated to Australia in the early 1960s from Munich in Germany was busy. Having fitted the mouthpiece over the man's mouth so there was no direct contact, Rudi was giving him the 'kiss of life' while I applied cardiac compression.

We were swiftly running out of time to save him when Rudi saw numbers tattooed on his arm, compliments of a World War II Nazi concentration camp in Germany. In a stroke of inspiration, Rudi shouted in his ear in German: 'Come on number 661266! Breathe! Come on damn it, breathe NOW!'

A shudder went through the man's body and, with a huge gasp, he was back with us, but not in any shape to see the end of the movie. Rudi turned to me with a surprised look on his face and said, 'See, he just needed to be ordered about.'

We kept the man going for the next two hours until we landed in Bangkok, where an ambulance and medico were waiting for us. Strapped on a stretcher wearing a full-face oxygen mask, the Jewish gentleman thanked us with his eyes as he was being whisked past us at the aircraft door.

'Another satisfied customer,' I said wryly, grinning at Rudi.

'Yes, and these bigger planes are bringing more and more of these sick people on board.'

The airline didn't bother to thank us.

42. Johno's One-and-only Call

Johno loved anything to do with horses, especially racing, and he was a mad gambler. He once told me that if he owned a racehorse he would keep it in his lounge room. I half believed him. He was one of the old chief stewards who had been flying for over thirty-five years and was coming up for retirement.

He had an act he sometimes did in crew-rooms around the world that amused the crew. He could call from memory famous races such as the Melbourne Cup, Silver Slipper, Caulfield Cup or even the English Derby. Pretty remarkable. All the horses' names, sometimes up to a dozen, were called, their jockeys, colours and handicaps spoken with the nasal voice that all race callers seem to have.

Included was all the fancy jargon callers used ... cut the first turf (they're off), on the journey (the race), the best view (in front), London to a brick on (the odds), the shillelagh (the whip), more rump in front than a butcher's shop (last), the pilot (jockey), hanging about like a cheap suit (in the middle) and thrown out the anchor (slowed down). When he retired he hoped to break into this vocation, doing country race calls.

His chance came one sunny Saturday afternoon in the country town of Tamworth, northern New South Wales, when by chance he ran into an old mate who was calling the races that day. His friend generously gave Johno his chance on a simple five-horse race — easy peasie.

Johno told me he was ecstatic at this chance — until they put the microphone in front of him and he went completely blank ... We never again heard race calls in the crew-room, and then he retired.

A good ten years went by. There at Royal Randwick Racecourse was Johno, all spruced up including a pork-pie hat with striped band. I asked him how he was going, and no, he was not calling races — the dream never happened. Too many people knew of his first call. Poor old Johno had a window-cleaning business.

43. Dangly Bits

Servicing of each aircraft was done on a strict schedule. After so many flight hours, a major overhaul was carried out. During one of these overhauls, a ground engineer thought he would improve the appearance of the kangaroo painted on the tail of the aircraft. He thought it looked a bit 'doctored'. What he did was paint on the logo two large testicles hanging down underneath the flying kangaroo's tail.

That aircraft was checked out and was flying around the world for almost a month before it was noticed. All hell broke loose, with Management wanting someone's scalp. After an intensive inquiry, no one was found, and wisely, no one owned up.

44. Infernal Horn

Ever been to Cairo in Egypt? If you have, the first thing that hits you coming out of the airport terminal is the chaotic traffic and constant horn blowing.

Our captain had a hell of a migraine on arrival one time, and was not looking forward to the crew bus trip to take us to our accommodation at the Hilton Hotel, right on the banks of the River Nile. He stopped to speak to the driver who sat behind the steering wheel with blood-shot eyes and a cigarette dangling from his lip.

'Driver,' the captain said in a persuasive voice, 'I've got a hell of a headache, so can you please refrain from blowing that infernal horn?' adding, 'I'll bet you an Egyptian pound to nothing you can't resist blowing it somewhere on the journey.'

We took off at a fast rate, dodging through the traffic, swerving around horse-drawn drays, and surprisingly coming to a squealing stop outside the hotel. The captain, who was always allowed to get off first, stopped beside the driver and, commending him on his restraint of not using the horn, handed over the pound note. The driver studied the captain before saying, 'Infernal horn broken!'

45. Hitman

At Bangkok Airport years ago we were always parked way down near the cargo building — I suspect because it was cheaper. The traffic officer would take us down to the aircraft in an open World War II-jeep-style transport. Sometimes, if we were only transiting through, it was required that we go to operations and sign in and out. One night, a steward signed the IN and OUT in green ballpoint and was arrested as, unbeknown to us, the only person in Siam (Thailand) permitted to use a green pen was the king. Lots of apologies and bowing got us out of it, with plenty of severe warnings.

On the night in question, I decided to walk down to where we were parked. The night was perfect — a soft breeze was blowing with that balmy warmth you only get in the tropics, and a sky full of stars once you got away from the brightly lit terminal. Halfway down I came across what I thought was a duffle bag that must have fallen off a baggage truck. When I got closer I discovered it was a man of about fifty who was dead. The body was in a terrible state, with a multitude of injuries. I hailed a passing catering truck, and the driver diverted to the terminal to let authorities know while I stayed with the body.

The inquiry that followed concluded that he was one of our disembarking passengers who had fallen out of the open door of the old bus used by the airport at that time, and then been run over by someone else. Leaving the terminal once again, I observed the three traffic officers drawing straws to see who was going to tell the relatives waiting outside. He had survived the flight, but not the transit bus to the terminal.

46. 472 years

From time to time, the company put on one-day seminars to bring us up to date on service, catering and how to improve the in-flight service. We were required to wear our uniforms and bring passports and vaccination books for appraisal. We all hated these days.

This seminar was for chief stewards only, and some of the chiefs who had been flying between thirty and thirty-five years were getting hot under the collar with some young office worker telling them how to suck eggs. Things were heating up when in rushed the cabin crew manager, saying a crew was running out of flight hours, there were no standbys left, and would any of the chiefs like to volunteer to passenger to Fiji, leaving in forty minutes, to bring the flight home.

There was a stampede to get our names down. Sixteen lucky chiefs were selected on seniority and, incredibly, I was last with twenty-one years of service. The flight home was only four hours and turned into a complete nightmare. The chiefs may know everything about silver service, but knew next-to-nothing of running economy class.

It was a very relieved crew who arrived back in Sydney, hoping none of the passengers complained. Combined years of service on that flight, including the technical crew, was a whopping 472 years. It was surely a record never to be beaten.

47. Zeb's Last Fling

When we stayed in Fiji, our accommodation was at the Mondo Cane Hotel/Motel. In its employ was a large, likable fellow called Zeb who was in charge of the pool bar and the area surrounding it. He was always smiling and laughing, kept the place spotless, and was a big asset to the hotel.

He had a little trick he would sometimes do when there were people lying about by the pool. With his round fibreglass waiter's tray, he would casually walk to the end of the pool. Then, with a quick flick of the wrist, he would send the tray spinning down the length of the pool, judging it just right so he could retrieve the bobbing tray at the other end.

Surely this was dangerous — it was! It was a glorious

sunny day when I saw Zeb head down to the pool end and let fly with the tray. It skipped across the water two or three times before a puff of wind lifted it airborne. At that precise moment a very British tourist, about sixty years old and dressed in a safari suit, was strolling by and, with a loud bong, the tray hit him on the head, sending him sprawling into a rhodenedron bush. The tray carried on, crashing through into the restaurant to the amazement of the customers there.

Within seconds, hotel staff were at the British man's side, wondering where the tray had come from. Zeb was a hundred metres away, busy unloading and carrying suitcases from the newly arrived tourist bus into the hotel, totally ignoring the drama by the pool. His good luck held that day as there were about twenty crew from different airlines, but not one of them blew the whistle on Zeb, who promptly gave up his little act.

48. Learning the Age-old Game

As I was walking down a back street in Calcutta, India, one sunny afternoon, I came across a group of twelve-year-old boys sitting in a row up against a fence. About an hour later, returning the same way, I noticed the boys were still sitting there.

When I approached them, one boy struggled to his feet and I was appalled to see him extract a short piece of broomstick screwed to a wooden base from up his backside.

'What on earth are you doing?' I exclaimed.

The boy proudly told me in his sing-song voice that they were enlarging their anuses so they could become male prostitutes. The world is full of surprises.

49. Chamber of Fools

When I joined the airline in the early 1960s we were legally required to become accredited in emergency procedures (EPs), which included ditchings in the pool, floating around in life rafts, using fire extinguishers and oxygen bottles, and taking a written exam at the end of each year. Then we all trooped out to Richmond Airforce Base in the bus to do, as we called it, the Chamber of Fools.

This was actually a decompression chamber and the exercise was to show us the effects of decompression on passengers and crew. The chamber was between two Nissen hangars and made of concrete in the shape of a large igloo about three metres across. There were circular windows set all around so those outside could observe what effects decompression had on the body — and boy oh boy it was very enlightening — and scary.

Those inside were subjected to slow decompression, and given simple tests to do such as add ten plus ten or write their names in chalk on a board. Technical and cabin crew alike would ponder over these simple tests. I saw a crew member write 'ten plus' in huge letters on the floor, and later refused to believe it was him.

Yes, I think they should still be doing the Chamber of Fools. It was very sobering.

50. Hoppy's Shooters

Because I frequently flew into San Francisco, California, over the years I got to know Police Officer Stan Fox pretty well. Everybody called him Hoppy (behind his back, that is), short for 'Hoppalong Cassidy'.

His beat as a foot patrolman was the tough Union Square area and he was damned good at his occupation. No matter what the weather, he was out there walking about, keeping a lookout for potential trouble, which he was always quick to rectify. It was funny to see the hookers, hoods, lowlifes, deadbeats and conmen fading into dark corners or running the other way as he strolled about. Of course he saw them, but until they broke the law they were entitled to walk the streets as much as he was. That was his philosophy.

The police were issued black uniforms, metal badges

and leather jackets; the firearms were standard issue, or fancier ones could be purchased at the individual officer's expense.

Stan was short and thick-set with sandy-coloured hair, looking a little like Alan Ladd, an actor in old Western movies. I often wondered if Hoppy was trying to portray the look of the modern-day peacemaker or sheriff. He walked the streets like a one-man taskforce with a two-way radio clipped to his belt next to the long, mahogany riot baton, handcuffs, bullets, night watchman's torch, and twin pearl-handled six-shooters nestled in non-regulation gun-fighter holsters.

Around the corner from the old Drake Hampshire Hotel where we stayed was a Bavarian-style beer hall. One side of this hotel was next to a pawn shop with all manner of electrical appliances, watches, jewellery and musical instruments haphazardly jumbled in the window behind sturdy steel mesh. On the other side was a gun shop with a neon sign in the window blinking on and off, which read, Go on, have fun — buy a gun.

The bar inside Bernie's beer hall was furnished with trestle tables, heavy exposed oak beams and with 'oomp-pa-pa' music playing non-stop. The barmen wore lederhosen national costume — short leather pants, braces, red-and-white striped shirts and jaunty alpine hats. The crew made Bernie's their drinking hole while in port as they not only sold five different brands of beer but the food menu also boasted great soups, stews and baked dinners.

Most nights Stan came in, checking around for wrong-doers. It was here that I got to know him; me with a beer, he with a coffee, sitting and yarning.

One summer evening, sitting at a table with the bar almost deserted, he unexpectedly drew out one of his Smith & Wesson specials. He twirled it expertly around his finger, then with a flick, turned it around so that the butt faced me. He said, 'Ever held a .45, Brian?' and indicated for me to take it. Truly, this was an honour. Taking the revolver carefully in my hand, I was surprised at how heavy it was, and wondered what the recoil would be. It was beautifully balanced; the finish on the steel was a dark blue, complementing the pearl handles that featured horse-heads carved into them. The long octagonal barrel was elaborately engraved and the bore was large enough for the handler to insert a little finger. Turning the gun over and admiring it, I observed an engraving on the base of the handle which read, 'Hoppy's Shooters'. Startled, I looked up into his smiling blue eyes. He knew! It was clear that he was not liked by crooks and drug-runners, but nobody wanted to go up against Stan and those shooters.

Several months later, drizzling rain was falling on a cold winter night when I hurried to Bernie's, ordered a Lucky Lager and settled down to watch a boxing match on the large TV screen mounted over the bar. I hoped

Stan had not done his rounds of the bar yet as I loved listening to his simple stories. For example, when he was directing heavy traffic on Mission Street, a smartly dressed, dignified-looking woman strode out to where he was standing and said, 'How nice to see police out doing point duty.'

'Thanks, lady,' he replied, thinking he was being complimented.

'While you're standing here, the banks are being f***ing robbed, women are being f***ing raped, and the streets are full of f***ing muggers. Well done,' she said sarcastically, marching off, leaving him open-mouthed.

Sipping the beer, I casually looked about the bar, then asked the barman, 'Has Stan been in yet?'

The barman stopped cleaning the bar top, gave me a sideways look and answered sadly, 'Haven't you heard what happened to Hoppy?'

'No, what happened to him?' I asked, not liking the way the barman was fidgeting about.

'He went and got himself killed.'

'Killed?'

'Some gang with a grudge lured him into the alley out the back by banging the trash cans about. When he went down to take a look, they jumped him,' the barman said with sad eyes. 'The cowardly bastards skewered him through the chest with a fourteen-inch (thirty-five cm) engineer's file, pinning him to the back door of the bar, and leaving him to die.'

I sat there stunned, the beer forgotten half way to my lips. The barman went down to serve another customer and on the way back stopped and said, 'Yeah, they also took his shooters.'

51. Marian

On the way to the hotel in London after a night flight from Bahrain one sunny spring morning, the crew bus pulled up at a red traffic light in busy Kensington. As we sat there in a jet-lagged state, a lady sitting at the window of a house opposite with red flowering geraniums in a window box caught my eye. The sun was streaming down, framing her in its golden light while all about her was in shade. It was only by chance that we were there when the sunlight happened to be at that angle. Five minutes either way and I would not have noticed her. I raised my hand, giving her a friendly wave. She immediately waved back, her face lit by a huge smile. Then the bus lurched forward, taking me out of her life, or so I thought.

The next time through London three weeks later, we stopped at the same traffic lights and again we waved to each other. This went on for about a year, with other crew catching on and also waving as they passed by. I was to hear later how it had spread to other airline crews, as the various bus drivers told them what we did, and they also began waving to her, accompanied by a beep of the bus horn.

I had arranged to be in London at a particular time as there was a special exhibition at a Kensington museum, which I was very keen to see. After spending a pleasant morning studying the fine display, I left the museum wondering where to have lunch. It occurred to me I was only a few blocks from the lady at the window.

I strolled down past the familiar set of traffic lights. There she was, so I waved. She was overcome with joy at the simple street visit and she beckoned me to come in. Across the road I entered a tiny, well-maintained garden ablaze with colour, lush green grass and trimmed hedges. The three-storey building was pure Victorian in red brick with contrasting white-pointed cement — obviously once the residence of a wealthy aristocrat, now divided into a rabbit warren of small flats.

The green front door of her flat was slightly ajar and she called out in a voice full of emotion, 'Do come in and have some tea. I'm dying to talk to you.'

It was a large room with a high, patterned plaster ceiling, a magnificent polished hearth and half-panelled oak walls — most likely the drawing room in bygone days. The effect was now spoilt by the makeshift kitchen in one corner and a neatly made bed in another. Cracks were zig-zagging down from the ceiling to the oak panelling like streaks of lightning, causing the wallpaper to split. The room was cluttered with expensive-looking, out-of-date furniture, but brightened by a rug that appeared to be Persian.

Marian was sitting by the window.

'G'day, my name is Brian,' I said, entering the flat.

'How nice to meet you after so many times passing by ... and oh, to hear that accent again after so long! Do come in and sit down,' she entreated me.

Marian was in her late sixties. Her hair, although a dark brown, was showing silver threads running through it. She must have been a very beautiful woman when young because she was still most attractive even though she had been, I was soon to learn, through hard times.

She was sitting in a wheelchair with a tartan rug around her legs. My eyes must have revealed my surprise. That's why she sits at the window all day, I thought.

Marian quietly said, 'Yes Brian, I'm crippled and have been ever since the blitz raids on London during the war. Do you remember any of it?'

I leaned back into the lounge chair and thought of the outback Australian town where we had lived when I was a kid, and how life during the years of World War II had gone on as usual.

'No, the only thing that sticks in my memory is Hitler's hysterical speeches on the radio. I remember there was a muddy air-raid trench meandering down the middle of the main street which my brother and I played in after school. But besides that, no, the war was far away.'

Gazing misty-eyed out the window, Marian picked up the threads of her story. 'I was engaged to be married during the war to an Australian pilot who came from Brisbane, and he spoke just like you. Max went on a bombing raid over Frankfurt on the 10th of May 1944 and never returned.'

'What a waste it all was,' I said.

'Two days later,' Marian continued, lost in the past, 'our house in Uxbridge on the outskirts of London was hit by a stray bomb, killing my whole family except me, and I got this.' She tapped her legs, and with a crooked smile, her blue eyes brimming with tears, she sighed and said, 'I never got to Australia.'

We chatted for about an hour over tea she served in willow-pattern china. She told me how difficult it was, her family gone, old friends dead or having lost contact with her, and Kensington was not exactly the easiest place to strike up friendships. In fact, it turned out she had practically no communication with anyone.

'It's terribly hard meeting other people. You have me now as a mate, Marian. I'll drop in each time I'm here in London. I'll so look forward to it.'

'Please do, Brian, that would be grand. People only rent here for a short time before moving on ...' Her voice trailed off.

'Well, now you have me as a cobber.' I explained that 'cobber' is the Australian slang for 'mate'.

We became good mates after that, and I shared stories of my travels around the world as we drank tea together.

On a blustering, windy spring morning, with buds sprouting on the bare trees, the crew bus motored past Marian's place, and I was concerned to see the frayed Holland blind was fully drawn down on her window.

'Stop the bus,' I shouted. Running across the road, I jumped the low hedge to see a black silk bow pinned on her door.

Just then, an Indian Sikh in native costume was coming down the corridor from his flat at the rear.

'Hey, mate, what's happened here? Is Marian okay?'

'My goodness, I'm telling you it is not good,' he said in a sing-song voice and back-to-front English. Shaking his head from side to side, he continued, 'Indeed she would be having a stroke and died. The postman was finding her two days later in her wheeling chair, in her hand a koala bear. Her funeral she would be having yesterday.'

I dreaded going past that intersection from then on; whereas before I hoped for a red light, now I fervently begged for it to be green. The place had fallen into disrepair; the window now painted a garish bright purple and a broken-down car on house bricks residing in the weed-infested grass.

Winter passed, summer arrived, and nearing the corner, I could not believe my eyes — the old building had been demolished and it was being replaced with a self-serve petrol station.

52. Beach Shirts and Live Wires

The year was 1969. The aircraft was a 707. Destination: Singapore, Karachi, Cairo, Rome, London. The plane had just left the terminal building at Singapore and were trundling along down to the end of the airfield for take-off when things changed dramatically. Serving orange juice to the economy-class passengers, I came to seat 46D, an aisle seat near the rear of the plane. As I attempted to hand him his juice, the passenger indicated towards his hands, which at first glance were just resting in his lap. It was then I saw his index finger holding red and black wires taped apart, sticking out of his long-sleeved shirt. With sad eyes he simply said, 'If I join these wires together, we all meet our Maker.'

Funny, but you would think my first reaction would have been — we are all going to die. No — that hit hard later. My immediate reaction was, I'm going to really earn my pay because safety is the main reason cabin crew are there, not serving drinks and food.

Slowly, I sat down on the armrest opposite and thought, What do you say to a maniac? Maybe, 'Well, who's going to win the footy on Saturday?' I honestly don't know what I said. Thankfully, Jesse, a level-headed steward, was passing and with my eyes I indicated the man's hands. I watched as he walked — not running — up the front and onto the flight deck. Good, they know.

The aircraft slowed down and then came to a stop, the maniac not noticing and carrying on about nobody loving him. The rear door opened and two huge security men appeared with Jesse pointing at me. As serious as the situation was, I almost smiled at the outlandish shirts the security men had borrowed as a disguise.

They silently came down the aisle and one got into the vacant seat behind the maniac. At a signal, the man behind grabbed him while the other jumped forward past me and karate-chopped the man's arm, with a loud crack — it was obviously broken.

They carted him down the back and threw him out of the door, tumbling down the steps onto the tarmac. More breaks, I hoped harshly, followed by his cabin bag. His suitcase was located in the hold and we were away two hours late. No slackening or counselling in those days.

A week later I was back in Singapore and enquired from the traffic officer what had happened to the man. He told me the bomb squad had taken him over by the perimeter fence, stripped off all his clothes and found electrical wires wound around and around his body with no explosives — the ends of the wire, incredibly, were stuck into the crack of his bum.

It turned out he had a grudge against the airline with no explanation for his action. Maybe he didn't get his window seat! He was transported to Greenway House (the asylum) and looked like being there for some time.

53. Boy, Oh Boy — What a Lady!

She was stacked. Boy oh boy. She was really buxom. Beautiful too. Not that painted-on kind of beauty, no siree. She was a natural beauty and, with these two qualities plus her acting ability, she'd become famous throughout the world.

The long night flight from Honolulu, Hawaii, was nearly over with just under half an hour to go before arrival at Sydney's International Terminal. Getting out of her aisle seat at the front of first-class, she stretched herself with her arms over her head, then reached up into the overhead locker. All the male passengers in first-class nearly had heart attacks looking at her magnificent bod.

She headed for the toilet carrying a zipped-up suit pack, obviously to change into something more appropriate before running the gauntlet of the notorious Australian news media at the airport.

Deep in concentration as I filled out the customs form on the bar top, I became aware of a soft 'psst'.

Looking about, everybody seemed to be content, when a more persistent 'PSST' made me look towards the first-class toilets. A hand and one blue eye were visible through the slightly open door, the hand's index finger beckoning me over. I nearly broke a leg getting there in two seconds flat.

She was dressed in the most splendid gown, what there was of it, hugging her every curve. It was made of some kind of metallic material, glittering in many shades of burnished gold. It was sensational! I thought, If she was going to wear this spectacular dress it was going to cause a riot as she walked to the terminal, shimmering in the morning sunlight. They had better call out the army.

In her deep voice, she asked me, 'Would you mind zipping me up?'

Wow, would I mind? I'll tell my grandchildren about it! She turned around and indicated the zip at the small of her back. 'You'll have to pull it real hard, Brian,' she giggled. As she took a huge breath, I grabbed the zipper in one hand, the back of her dress in the other, thinking, this is going to be mission impossible, as I gave it a good yank. To my horror there we were, both looking bug-eyed at the zipper. I'd pulled it completely off the dress!

I'll say one thing for her, she was a cool customer; not only beautiful with a fantastic figure, but she also with a sense of humour. She didn't say things like, 'You clumsy clown', or 'You stupid oaf'. She simply said,

'That's torn it'. A row of eight safety-pins, hastily, and with great difficulty, fastened it as best as I could, with her giggling the whole time.

It was rather chilly when the front door of the aircraft was flung open. She had come prepared in case of inclement weather, putting on a cape made of the same fantastic material. As she was leaving, she stopped when she got to me and, with a wink, said in her deep, sexy voice, 'You naughty boy, Brian,' and handed me the zipper. The cameramen's tongues were dragging on the ground as she strutted her stuff in four-inch- stiletto-heeled shoes across the airport. A trifling little thing like eight safety-pins holding her dress together was nothing to worry about!

54. Bay Rum and Mirror Man

Many years ago, out the front of the old, columned Colonial Metropole Hotel on the busy corner of Northbridge Road in Singapore was Lee Wang's hairdressing salon. Wang didn't have any rental problems because his business was on the footpath. The set-up consisted of an old barber-style chair that I strongly suspect originally came from a dentist's surgery. This suspicion was strengthened by the still-attached porcelain bowl now used for washing the shaving brush.

His antique tools of trade resided in a well-worn Gladstone bag by his feet. But boy, could he cut hair! I always went around to Wang's to have a trim when in 'Singas', and after he was finished, he would splash on a hair tonic called Bay Rum, massaging it into the scalp and making my head tingle.

One day, he was busy rubbing the tonic in when a flash of light caught my eye. I turned my head in the direction of the street corner where the flash had come from, but whatever it was, it was gone. I turned back and there it was once more. Glancing around again I saw nothing. The next time I was ready, and was surprised to see that it was reflected sunlight coming from mirrors stuck onto and over the insteps of the shoes of a man standing nearby holding a small briefcase.

Wang was finished, but I was reluctant to leave. I wanted to find out why a man would be wearing mirrors on his shoes.

'The tonic is fifty cents extra, sir,' Wang interrupted, adding, 'How about a nice pair of sunglasses, chewing gum, coloured condoms or cigarettes?'

'Yeah, I'll take one,' I absent-mindedly told him, not taking my eyes from the mirror man.

'One cigarette, one condom or one pair of sunglasses?' Wang asked patiently.

Just then, a young, attractive woman strutted up to the mirror man and, after a brief discussion, he slid his foot between her legs, intently peering down into the mirror. On such a crowded intersection, it was astonishing that nobody seemed to notice this man looking up the girl's short dress. He was a pox doctor!

After this novel examination, he dispensed some pills from his briefcase, a few dollars were exchanged, and the girl departed to spread more 'gifts of joy'. In no time at all another girl was asking for advice, then another and another. He has a regular little business going here for the night fighters from the nearby back streets and, I thought to myself, like Wang, he had no rent to pay.

The Metropole, Lee Wang, the pox doctor and the girls of the night are all gone now due to the building of a better city. Now, cigarette smoking is frowned on, chewing gum is illegal, but condoms are highly recommended. That's progress, I guess. But the intrigue and fascination, the unexpected and the old-world charm have suffered on account of it, as in so many other places around the world.

55. My Goodbye

Living near or under the flight path of jet airliners can be a harrowing existence. We lived under the flight path, but thankfully a few miles from the airport. At least the aircraft had a bit of height as they thundered over our house to far-away destinations. Each time I took off on a flight I would intently look down on our house as it passed under the starboard wing, looking for the goodbye sign.

One day, I happened to be travelling as a passenger to Singapore to replace a steward who had become ill there. Sitting in an aisle seat, I was straining my neck to look down on the old house. The business man seated beside me in the window seat was watching me as I looked with absorbed concentration over his shoulder.

'What's so interesting?' he asked me.

'See that tall, red-brick office building down there on the main road?' I replied, not taking my eyes off the ground.

'Yes, I've got it,' the man said.

'Come back six houses to the white house with a tennis court in the backyard,' I said. 'That's my mum standing in the middle of the court, waving a tea towel.'

56. The Palmist

Before Pam flew, she worked the 'rattlers' to Dubbo, Bathurst and Grafton as a waitress in the dining car for the New South Wales Railways. She had a funny little habit that amused me each time we flew together, serving in the first-class cabin. I would catch her doing it, and suppress a smile. She would catch my eye and whisper, 'I must stop doing that,'

'Doing what?' I'd innocently reply.

Serving on the old, speeding steam trains, swaying about, the waitress would jam one leg up against the edge of the seat before placing the ordered food on the table so as not to be off balance. Pam was always doing this even when you could stand a coin on edge, as the aircraft was so smooth.

Julie was waiting for a taxi outside the old Seaview Hotel when Pam walked briskly out through the glass doors into the steamy noonday heat in Bangkok.

'Hello, Julie,' Pam said, smiling. 'Going shopping?'

Julie, looking embarrassed, replied, 'Oh, hi Pam! Well, no ... actually I'm going to have my fortune read.'

Intrigued, Pam asked if she could tag along and see the performance. She was visualising a gypsy woman gazing into a crystal ball in a darkened room, muttering things like, 'You will meet a handsome rich film star, have five kids and be happy ever after.'

'Only if you don't make fun of me or Abdul,' Julie said, interrupting Pam's thoughts. 'I go quite often to see him and, even though I don't believe a lot of what he tells me, he's mighty close on some things.'

The taxi dropped them off on the busy corner of Phaya Thai Road, and there, like many of the small businesses throughout Asia years ago, was Abdul the Palmist's footpath establishment. The site was well-chosen; situated between an open-fronted Thai restaurant unimaginatively called 'The Golden Pagoda' and a curry go-down, right on a bus stop. Passengers alighting from the bus, or diners from the restaurant or curry warehouse, all became potential customers for him. All around was the smell of diesel exhaust fumes combined with the sweet aroma of curry and the sizzling, appetizing dishes being cooked in large woks at the Golden Pagoda.

Abdul was sitting cross-legged on a battered tubular steel chair under a huge beach umbrella with 'Marlboro' stencilled around the edge, poring over a filthy, dog-eared book on astrology. He was an Indian from Bombay (as Mumbai was then called) and must have been around eighty years old; his body was stick-thin with distended veins standing out on his scrawny arms. He looked up and watched the girls approach with intelligent, 'seen it all', bright dark eyes like two buttons sunken deep into their sockets. Sticking out from under the full-length, striped gown were his feet, incongruously encased in a pair of new striped running shoes. It struck Pam that the footwear somehow spoilt the overall effect.

As the girls drew closer, he was busy running a grubby finger over a chart nailed to the brick wall that displayed a palm and all the intricate lines of fate, love, hope and death. The only two items in his outdoor office were a cane chair of indeterminate age, and a rickety, fold-up card table. Residing on the table were seven or eight books similar to the one he was reading, all in various stages of falling apart. Next to his elbow was a school exercise book full of notes, and a chewed pencil stub.

Totally oblivious to the noisy bedlam of the buses, hawkers, pedestrians and organised chaos in the Golden Pagoda, Abdul raised his thin arm above his head and beckoned them over. His old face broke into a huge, ghastly grin, displaying the only five teeth he had left, stained a dark red from the betel nut he constantly chewed. The area all around within spitting distance of his chair was stained from many years of the filthy substance being spat on the pavement. From a distance, the stains gave the illusion of him having laid out a motley red carpet.

'Sit, sit, missie,' Abdul sing-songed to Julie, wagging his turbaned head from side to side, indicating the cane chair. Reaching out, he took Julie's hand, turned it palm up and peered with deep concentration for so long that Pam was beginning to wonder if maybe he had popped off. Suddenly, he reached out for one of his books, thumbing through the pages. Ten minutes went by before he told Julie, what to Pam sounded like the usual drivel, to watch out for the tenth day of the month, that the problem with her lover was going to hot up, and to take particular care on any property investments. Delving into her cluttered handbag, Julie drew out a 50-baht note and held it out to Abdul, who put it in a chocolate tin with a portrait of Queen Elizabeth II at her coronation on the lid.

Abdul then swung his bright eyes to Pam, saying, 'Sit, missie.' Pam hesitated, then thought, Why not! It's only 50 Baht. Sitting down, she slid the money across the table. Taking her hand, Abdul sat looking at it for only a matter of seconds before quickly pushing her money back, saying, 'Very difficult. I can't see anything.'

Pam and Julie were both amazed at this answer.

'You must be able to see something.' Making light of the whole thing, Pam added, 'Am I going to marry someone who is rich?'

'I can't see anything!' Abdul persisted. Retrieving her money, Pam was puzzled by how nervous he had become. She put her money in her purse and rose to leave. Looking up sadly, the old man whispered to her, 'Be careful, missie. Beware of fire.'

Two things are the enemy of aircrew: one is crashes, which we don't talk about, and anyway, if it does happen, most crew members have resigned themselves to the fact that you either walk away from it or you don't. The second is fire on board. For instance, if your home catches fire you call the fire brigade and fight on, hoping that they will arrive quickly. Not so on an airliner; you could be three or four hours from the nearest airport, perhaps flying over ocean. We are all trained to fight fire, using every means available and all the latest fire-fighting equipment.

Pam didn't stay long flying after visiting Abdul and we thought it was due to what he had said. She married a lovely fellow who was a policeman and she became a housewife, living in an old-style block of flats without balconies on the top floor of a block overlooking Botany Bay.

The moon had not yet risen over the ocean and the night was dark — very dark. From out of the bushes the drugged-out pyromaniac slunk into the flats, carrying an armful of loose newspapers and cardboard, throwing it into the lift. Flicking a lit match onto the paper, he pressed the sixth-floor button and the automatic doors silently closed.

The sixth floor! Pam's floor! And she was home alone. The fire took hold very quickly in the old building and the first Pam knew of any danger was when she walked out of the kitchen where she was cooking dinner. The fire was devouring the unit's wooden entry door and, even while she stood frozen, it was progressing across the carpet. The intense heat made her reel back and climb out of the kitchen window onto a narrow ledge.

Her last words, clinging to a waste pipe caught in the glare of a spotlight from the fire engine that had just arrived, were, 'Tell Jim I love him.' The grasp she had on the now-glowing downpipe relaxed and she tumbled to the concrete driveway six storeys below.

'Be careful, missie. Beware of fire.'

57. Happy Birthday, Cardboard Box Babies

It was a hot, steamy afternoon in Bangkok on 4 April 1975. Sitting on a bar stool in the Grand Prix Bar & Grill situated in the notorious Patpong Road, I ordered another San Miguel beer and settled down in the semi-darkened room to watch a movie through the smoky haze.

With the first drink came a pair of earphones, which plugged into jacks that ran all the way along the top of the bar. This enabled patrons to follow the soundtrack of the movie being projected onto the grubby wall.

Now and then, the bat-wing doors would creak open, letting in the harsh sunlight and causing those inside to blink. The thirsty tourist or local (usually selling lottery tickets) would enter, and even the locals were apt to squint until their eyes adjusted to the dark.

I was unaware of the adventure shortly to follow when a crew member shouted out, 'There's Leary,' and I was pulled, headset and all, backwards off the bar-stool. There were ten other crew members with him, including a captain, all from different crews on layover in Bangkok. The captain's voice quavered as he asked me, 'Brian, we need you badly to make up a crew for an emergency flight to Sydney.'

'No way,' I quickly answered, banging my hand down on the bar for emphasis. Every two months, crew were entitled to bid for one trip of their choice and this was mine, with four lovely days in sunny Rome. 'I'm not giving that up for anything. Besides,' I argued, 'I've been drinking within flight regulations.'

The captain gravely answered, 'Let me explain the situation, Brian, then you can make your decision, okay?' He went on to reveal how Saigon in nearby Vietnam had been under attack during the war and a stray bomb had hit an orphanage on the outskirts of town, with disastrous consequences. Those who could make it were being evacuated by military aircraft out of the war zone to Bangkok Airport. The plane, after disembarking its human cargo, immediately returned to the war.

A plan was quickly formulated by the Australian government to accept the children as migrants. Doctors and nurses offered their services and an aircraft was found to bring the little ones 'home'. This was the emergency flight and reluctantly I agreed to join the crew, even though I was still sceptical and disappointed about those four days in Rome, until we arrived at the airport.

Inside the old hangar-like terminal building in the stifling heat, in various stages of dying, were the orphans of Saigon. There were kids with limbs missing, others horribly burned, and over half of them had killer and crippling diseases, and all the other injuries of war. The oldest child was about ten years old, and those who had miraculously escaped injury were sliding around the cracked tile floor on pieces of cardboard having a lovely time. One little fellow, crippled badly by polio, rode everywhere on his mate's back, all the way to Sydney.

Along one wall of the building was a row of cardboard shoe boxes. Casually walking over for a closer inspection, I was shocked to find little babies, only a few days old, dehydrating inside. Rome was forgotten.

It was obvious that even with some people from the Australian Embassy, there were not going to be enough hands onboard to cope with so many small, sick children. Sixteen local British Airways ground personnel jumped in to help, plus a ground hostess (all with no passports, change of clothes or anything) joining the flight of life to Sydney. On arrival in Australia, these wonderful helpers were not allowed to enter and they left again soon after for the long haul back to Bangkok. Bloody bureaucracy — they should have been allowed to rest for a day or two at least!

The doctors and nurses were busy examining each child and labelling them with their complaints written on suitcase bag tags. They all had identification straps on their tiny wrists stating their names in unpronounceable Vietnamese, so the doctors decided for the sake of expediency to identify them by their ailments.

This truly was an emergency. If we did not get these kids into the air-conditioned aircraft immediately and give them fluids and medication, we were going to lose them. Each of us carried a shoebox with the precious contents, and led the children who could walk into the aircraft, like pied pipers. Most of these children had never been outside the gates of the orphanage, let alone on a jet liner. The awe of the vast interior, plush seats and carpets, showed on their little faces. It was marvellous how children can put crises so quickly aside for the moment, even though deep down they were scared.

Meanwhile, the captain and technical crew were busy refuelling and servicing the plane. The doors were closed and we taxied to the end of the runway. Crew seats for take-off face backwards, not only because it is safer, but also so that the passengers' behaviour can be observed. What further stunned me, as I looked down the cabin from my seat at the front, was that it appeared to be deserted, so small were the passengers. The only people visible were the helpers, doctors and nurses scattered about trying to calm those nearby strapped in seats and on the floor in cardboard boxes.

As soon as the 'fasten seat-belts' sign went off, Mel, a fellow steward, and I dived into the galley where we spent the next eight hours. Using tongs, Mel dunked baby bottles and teats into boiling water and poured a dessertspoonful of baby formula into each bottle, which was then handed to me for filling with warm milk. No sooner was one bottle filled than we started on an empty one. No time for meals or cups of tea. No time for anything except keeping these kids alive.

Along the aisles, the doctors, nurses and crew fought

to keep the little ones alive; feeding, cleaning and administering medications. Nappy-changing went on non-stop. The soiled ones were thrown into large plastic bags until the latter ran out, then they were thrown loose into the rear toilets. The stench was unbelievable. Amidst these appalling conditions, the older children, more or less in a healthy state, thought it was wonderful being busy with colouring books and crayons or chasing one another around the aircraft.

The upstairs lounge, usually reserved for the use of first-class passengers having cocktails, was cordoned off as an intensive care area, and on these luxurious velour seats three little ones were fighting for their lives. Just before sunset, the aircraft touched down at Mascot. The captain (well aware of his precious cargo) made the smoothest landing of his career. All the orphans were still alive, although some were far from well.

When the aircraft door was thrown open, it revealed the assembled media, medical staff, police and airport authorities waiting on the apron. To make the most of the occasion, the airline had quickly found the three prettiest ground hostesses on duty to walk up the stairs to the plane as the TV cameras rolled. To our amusement, the girls only got halfway up when the stench hit them and they retreated in haste. We uglies, in our dirty, smelly uniforms, took over at this point and delivered the orphans to the waiting ambulances.

These poor children at last got a lucky break. They

were all adopted and became citizens of Australia, the Lucky Country.

I sometimes wonder what they are doing, where they work and where they are living. Are the older ones married with little ones of their own, and are they happy? May God bless you, wherever you are, Cardboard Box Babies.

58. Welcome to Vietnam

During the late 1960s and early 1970s, the Vietnam War was in full swing and 707 troop charters were being flown from Sydney to Saigon by volunteer crews. The Australian Army had it well organised and camouflaged the departures of these flights by allowing the troops to arrive at the airport and board the aircraft in 'civvies'. This low-profile attitude was adopted because of the demonstrations, burning of draft cards, and the general reaction to this most unpopular war.

These troop flights were under the supervision of an officer who maintained order and saw to it that no liquor of any kind was served to the soldiers. An hour out of Saigon, the commanding officer made an announcement over the PA, ordering the troops to remove their 'civvies' and put on their military uniforms.

'Time to go to war,' he concluded.

Up to this point, the flight was rather relaxed, with lots of the young lads having never been in an aircraft before. The captain made it known that all were welcome to come up to the flight deck for a 'look see'.

With the soldiers' uniforms on, the flight took on a tense atmosphere. The lumbering 707 was escorted into the airfield by fighter aircraft, flying close in off each wing tip, while gunships hovered on the perimeter. It was not unusual for snipers to open fire on us as we descended for the landing, the target being pretty hard to miss.

One time, the enemy set up a mortar firing a barrage of shells, forcing the captain to take evasive action, veering steeply off to port. It must be remembered this was a Boeing 707, which did not manoeuvre well. In fact, it flew like a house brick. The airport sent out troops to rout the enemy while we flew around and around, watching the battle from a dress-circle seat. Welcome to Vietnam!

We stayed there for several hours, before loading up with another batch of troops who had done their tour of duty and were going home. Some of the soldiers had married while there and their brides were also on board. It was a different scene. The bars were open and a party soon began at 40,000 feet, with tensions relaxed, their fighting done, but best of all they were going home. Yet, in all the flights I did, I can't recall even one incidence of rudeness or unsociable behaviour from the young men. Well done, boys.

59. Cardboard Box Baby Reunion

Twenty years passed by and out of the blue I received a phone call from Channel 9. They said they had been contacted by Zion, one of the cardboard-box babies, enquiring if they knew of anyone from that mercy flight. They found me.

As Qantas was celebrating its seventy-fifth anniversary, Channel 9 decided to do an episode of 'This Is Your Life' on this (yet another historic occasion). Zion and I were as the main features.

A handsome, fit, tanned young man walked over to me on the set of Channel 9 and said, in the broadest Aussie accent, 'G'day, Brian, how yer goin'?'

Zion told me he was now playing tennis professionally. Not bad after nearly dying in a cardboard shoe box. He was also now married to a lovely Vietnamese lady.

They also found the little lad who had ridden on his mate's back on 'that' flight. He has had his experiences published and has his own photography business.

I contacted a club in Cabramatta, NSW, which has a large community of Vietnamese people, and spoke to a lady there. She told me that for the past twenty years they had held a get-together for these kids, and had just held the final one as the 'babies' had all grown up and were dispersed all over Australia. She explained that it was like the population of a small town — some studying to be doctors, dentists, firemen, etcetera; others had crossed paths with the law, some were alcoholics and so on. Life is indeed strange.

60. Surviving Against All Odds

Each year in August, the Blue Mountains town of Springwood, NSW, celebrates the Battle of Long Tan, which took place during the Vietnam War. As I walked along the footpath in my uniform, wearing my medals and heading for the pub and the reunion, a beautiful lady stopped me. She was aged in her fifties and was dressed in Vietnamese national costume. She gestured for us to sit down on a bench in the main street. Here is the story she told me.

When Saigon, in South Vietnam, fell to the North (communists and the Viet Cong), the country was full of roving soldiers looking to cause trouble. They stormed into her home, shot her mother, father and elder brother dead. She was thrown naked out into the street and the house burned down. She was just five years old. In a flash — she had no family, no home, no clothing — nothing. How on earth do you forgive or recover from that? She tried to smile, although her lips quivered and tears flowed down her cheeks. We walked arm-in-arm down to the reunion. I see her there each year and we silently hug each other, remembering.

61. And Then the Sun Came Out

Lightning streaked across the early morning sky, accompanied by deafening claps of thunder, with the rain coming down in sheets, bouncing off the tarmac and flooding the apron area. As I looked out of the terminal window, I thought to myself, You have to be slightly mad to fly for a living, but to fly in this weather is almost mentally certifiable.

Just then, the public address system crackled into life with a bored Australian voice informing passengers on Flight 27 to Auckland New Zealand, that it was delayed due to mechanical problems.

'Great, just bloody great!' I mumbled to nobody in particular. This was the perfect cocktail for a planeload of grumpy, irritable, apprehensive passengers, and I wondered just what mechanical problem it was anyway. Eventually, after a two-hour wait, the flight was called and the people huddled under airline umbrellas, dodged puddles, and scuttled to the aircraft parked — wouldn't you know it — way out from the terminal. This was not going to assist in improving their tempers or humour. I should have stayed home in bed.

The flight to Auckland took one hour and fifty minutes and the crew worked flat out, no time for chatting. In first-class, it was first drinks and hot savouries all round, then lay up the tables and serve a full seven-course meal, including carved beef, from the trolley. There was never enough time, with coffee, liqueurs and the stowing of equipment still going on when the wheels went down, signalling to us that we had roughly five minutes until landing.

I hope this flight goes well. First-class was full with twenty passengers, among them the aloof Sir John and Lady Wilkins, Frederick McCarthy (a prominent barrister), a member of parliament from New Zealand, and Mr Thomas, an executive from the Boeing Corporation. The rest were business people and a honeymoon couple. The last first-class passenger to board, dressed in an outlandish checked suit and pork pie hat, full of fun, with laughter in his eyes, was an African-American comedian.

After take-off, he came out to the galley and said, with a glint in his eye, 'Let's stir these poor, morbid, gloomy souls up. Do you mind if I act as the chief steward for a bit?'

'Sure,' I answered. 'Here, take my jacket and bow tie,' helping him put them on. The jacket reached just below his waist and looked ridiculous. I thought he planned on doing a short skit, then hand the meal service back to me. Wandering out beyond the curtain, I was surprised to see he had the seating plan and was moving everyone about.

Holy smoke! He had Lady Wilkins sitting next to the man weighing about 115 kg with an unkempt beard and drinking beer out of a can. The barrister was moved in with the honeymooners' bride. Mr Thomas of Boeing got stuck with an unlikely companion; and staid old Sir John ended up in the back seat having a lovely time with the best-looking sort on board.

The comedian then proceeded to give them one of his finest performances all the way to New Zealand, with me on the other end of the traymobile. We only got as far as the coffee course with him, all the while messing around, before the wheels went down for landing.

We arrived at the Auckland terminal and the first-class passengers all got off laughing. Mr Thomas remarked to me that a Boeing aircraft has never seen a meal like that before, and Sir John was grinning from ear to ear as well.

Last to get off was the comedian, who thanked me for letting him do what he enjoyed most — making people laugh. I found out later he had done this caper on other airline flights. The sun was shining in Auckland.

62. The Turtle

The passengers were strolling across the apron to the aircraft at Manila International Airport with the usual load of locally made wood carvings, straw handbags, crocheted tablecloths, and Manila rum brewed about a week ago. The big, crew-cut, smart-aleck Australian ascended the stairs, stopped and, without any form of a hello, thrust a large turtle shell made into a hideous lamp into my hands, saying, 'Look after this, buddy, and make sure it doesn't get broken.'

'I wish I could put it back on the turtle,' I tersely replied. It must have been over 100 years old. Albie, the local traffic officer standing next to me, was staring at the shell with grief in his eyes, appalled that some idiot would do such a thing and that someone just as stupid would want to buy it.

'It's too big for the cabin, Albie,' I said. 'Can you find somewhere to stow it in the hold?'

Albie took it in his arms, gently stroking the shell, a half-smile on his face as he walked away. The last sighting of the turtle (minus the electrical bits) was with Albie walking over to an area behind the water tanks at the back of the terminal. He had the shell tucked under one arm and a long-handled shovel in the other.

63. Customs

Many years ago, when the terminal was on the other side of the airport at Kingsford Smith, Sydney, Australia, the customs hall was a long, narrow, fibro shed with a tin roof. Cold as charity in winter and hot as hell in summer, it was a cheerless place.

The customs officers complained about how cold it was in winter and large gas-fired heaters were installed in the ceiling rafters with a chain hanging down and a ring on the end to turn it on. Jesse and I entered the customs hall on a bright summer's morning, and Jesse, seeing the ring on the end of the chain, hung his coat cover on it.

After several minutes I was in the middle of saying, 'Can anyone smell gas?' when Jesse lit up a cigarette. The explosion was huge, with everybody running for the exit.

The next time I entered the hall, looking at the now-blackened ceiling, I casually asked the officer if they ever found out why it exploded.

'It's a bit of a mystery,' he replied.

Not to Jesse and me it isn't. Jesse left flying sometime later and joined the CIA.

Years ago, there was a flight engineer who, on arrival at Mascot Airport in Sydney, always seemed to have a garden hose slung over his shoulder to declare to customs. There is an old saying, 'Too much of a good thing...', and it applied to him. This particular day, an observant customs officer asked him why he needed so many garden hoses. Surely, he was not selling them, as the fittings were different and would not fit our taps.

The officer saw a cork pushed into the fitting and, when he removed it, out ran three litres of scotch whiskey all over the bench and floor.

*

It was interesting to observe the way crew packed their bags whenever there was a customs inspection; some were like a rat's nest and others were all laid out neatly. One thing I was very particular about was how I packed my shoes — always in a plastic bag. It was amazing how many of the crew just threw their footwear, which could have been walking the filthy back streets of Calcutta (now Kokata) or Karachi, or somewhere else the day before, on top of freshly laundered clothing.

One day, I was in line at customs behind the captain after arrival in Sydney from Singapore, waiting for an inspection. He threw open the lid of his bag and there, sitting on top, was the whole girlie thing of skimpy black bra, panties, suspender belt, negligée — the works. The customs officer, fingering one of the garments, looked up, and the captain said flippantly, 'You wear what you like, I'll wear what I like.'

At that moment, the main exit door opened and a gorgeous blonde lady, standing outside, waved to the captain. The customs officer saw her and said to the captain, 'Don't let me keep you, Sir. Next.'

*

Flying into Sydney's International Airport years ago, the crew of eleven trooped down to customs for inspection. On the left side was a long bench for crew only, and the customs officer stood right behind it. There was a large window looking out on the hall. The custom officers were unpredictable; one time waving us straight through, another time a full tip-out search. This day we were all standing around waiting by the bench, when out of the office marched three officers. They grabbed one of the crew and escorted him into the office. We all assumed he had some kind of contraband. This made us pretty nervous as most of us had small, undeclared things. In particular, enthusiastic trainee customs officers, when handling us, were over the top.

After about five minutes we were all cleared to leave. When we got into the crew bus, there was the fellow who had been taken into the office.

'What happened to you?' I asked.

'Nothing,' he said. 'They were too busy watching you lot through the one-way glass, doubled over laughing at you all trying to push the extra watch up your arms or whatever.' Customs did have a sense of humour!

64. Lost Property

Ever wondered what happened to that favourite dress, shirt, or jumper that suddenly went missing when you were on a trip? I returned to the hotel one sunny day in Tehran, Iran, to find the housemaid cleaning my room. There she was, caught red-handed, slipping my blue cashmere jumper under the mattress! Management became involved and under the proviso of her 'coming clean', the police would not be called. She admitted doing it, and said that she had quite often hidden things. Her defence was that it was not actually stealing as the hotel guest DID leave the article behind on departure. After all, airline staff and travellers alike check the wardrobe, bathroom — and now the mattress should be added as well.

About a year before this latest incident, I was walking in the same hotel's delightfully serene garden and stopped dead — there was my lost white American-college-style cardigan that my wife had knitted for me with two distinctive red bands on the left sleeve. It was in an appalling state with both elbows worn out and filthy. How the hell did the gardener end up with my cardigan? It makes me wonder. Did the housemaid have a nice little business going, with no outlay at all for 'lost' property?

65. The Eleventh Commandment

I should have known the moment I saw him that he would upset the system. He was a well-known American actor and singer. Short and chubby with a great deal of hair, like an explosion in a mattress factory. As I was handing out the menus, he approached me and said he belonged to a religious sect that forbade him to eat in public.

'Is there somewhere I can eat in private, maybe the crew-rest?'

Is this fellow having a joke with me? I thought.

'No,' I told him. 'You will have to eat in your first-class seat.'

'What about the toilets? Can I use one of them?' he asked.

'You have to be joking!'

I started the meal service, setting up the tables, tablecloth, cutlery, pepper, salt, serviettes and wine glasses. He gathered up his set and headed for the toilet, setting it all up on the tiny bench next to the sink, and crouched down on the toilet seat with a silly grin.

He's serious! Entrée going in, followed by wine, main, dessert, fruit, cheese, coffee, and nothing coming out. When we were finished serving the meal he reappeared, and on the way back to his seat he thanked me for the excellent service.

I looked in the toilet with plates, cutlery and food all over the bench top, sink and floor — it took me half an hour to clean it all up. Who was the nut who thought up this Eleventh Commandment: 'Thou shalt eat in the toilet'?!

66. Bluey

Hosties and stewards came from all walks of incredible life. Don was one of them. Before he joined up, he was a professional boxer and could really go the knuckle. He was also a big drinker. He was completely plastered in the crew-room in Tehran after many vodka-and-tonics before keeling over onto the floor, out cold. The crew referred to this action as 'kissing the carpet goodnight'.

A steward (who will remain anonymous to save his life) thought it would be a good joke to put a piece of blue vein cheese under Don's armpits. No amount of washing and deodorants could remove the smell for days, with Don on the warpath. Don got the nickname 'Bluey' after that, but never to his face.

67. Out-of-control Controllers

Ever wondered why sometimes you board an aircraft and can feel the crew are unwelcoming, surly or just plain unhappy? Don't blame the crew. If this happens, blame the cabin crew person in charge: purser, manager, supervisor, director, whatever they are called — some of these people should never have been employed, let alone put in charge of a crew. Many have no idea how to treat crew members and get the best out of them, picking out silly little things to complain about, never giving any encouragement or thanking the crew for a job well done after a long, hard flight. I suspect that these people have very little life other than flying, and it would not surprise me if they were taking their manual to bed with them.

There was a classic example of this many years ago on a long, eighteen-day trip to London and back, where an over-the-top supervisor, known for his 'nit-picking', had upset every crew member, including me (his 'right-hand man'), with his ridiculous, silly little games in the first sector on day one. The crew declared they had enough and, unless it was company or safety-related, he was 'not on board' — in other words, sent to coventry. His reply to this was that he would take me back to the office on our return for insubordination, to which the whole crew said they would all come. It was a very long, lonely flight all the way for him. Incidentally, it was quite common for these idiots to open their brief-cases in customs after a flight to find a melted ice-cream cake inside. By now, there will be a lot of smiling crew members reading this, and nodding their heads.

68. One-way Horse Riding

Horse riding was popular in Cairo. You could hire horses near Mena House and ride out across the desert like Lawrence of Arabia and down to Memphis (Sequoia).

What they didn't tell riders at the stables was (and I think they thought it a great joke) that when dismounting one should never let go of the reins of the horse or forget to tie the horse up — because if you didn't, the horse took off for home, leaving the poor rider with a five-mile or eight-kilometre walk back through soft sand.

They never sent anybody looking for such riders, and when they arrived back at the stables, there would be the horse, watered, fed, brushed down and, I reckon, laughing. Yes, it happened to me, but only once.

69. Siddy

The first time I met Siddy James, he was standing at the economy entrance door of the 707 with his hands on his hips and looking very bloody annoyed.

'Where the hell have you been?' he snapped at me.

I replied, 'Look, I'm late boarding because I've just had a dressing down from the cabin crew manager about that party in Tahiti, so give me a break.'

News of that party had spread like wildfire through the crew-rooms across the world. I had a front room with a huge balcony overlooking the beach in Tahiti. It started out as a quiet couple of drinks before dinner and escalated into a full-blown party, going on till the early hours. People came from everywhere. The only person on our crew not present was the captain, who was a teetotaller.

At call-time it was a motley crew who showed up in the foyer to fly to Sydney via Nandi, Fiji. The captain waited until we were all seated in the airline transport bus before he stood up and announced we were all going on report for disgusting and offensive behaviour. He said the disgraceful noise must have kept the whole hotel awake, himself included.

'You can all look forward to being demoted or suspended,' he concluded.

We were a worried crew on that flight until the

captain came down with malaria before we were to land in Fiji, and was offloaded on a stretcher to the hospital in Nandi.

The flight engineer didn't improve matters by saying as the captain was carried off, 'If you had had a few drinks, it would have killed the bugs.' By the time the captain got out of hospital and back to Sydney, it was old news and we all only got a slap on the wrist.

Anyway, back to Siddy.

Siddy calmed down after a while and we became good friends. He had a little trick that he did as he was standing, chatting with passengers in flight. He would reach into his pocket for the penny he carried and start intricately weaving it through his fingers. I asked him why he did it and he said he learned to do it in the German prisoner-of-war camp during World War II.

Siddy is gone now. I hope they remembered to put the penny in his hand before they buried him.

70. San Francisco (before Hank and Larry)

San Francisco is Sydney's American sister city, and whoever thought they were alike, apart from both of them being on a harbour, must have had rose-coloured glasses on or been on the funny smokes. Down-town appears at first glance to be rich and glamorous. There are many first-class, five-star hotels and new skyscrapers perched precariously on the steep hills, gleaming in the Californian sun. The pleasant sound of cable cars dinging their bells as they rumbled by, mingled with the excited chatter of tourists hanging onto the side, creates a happy atmosphere. Beautiful department stores with elaborate window displays and well-to-do apartments on Nob Hill all help to create this illusion. Most cities have a rough, rundown area, and San Francisco is by no means an exception.

Down on Market Street (lower) and Mission Street are where the bums, deros, conmen, criminals, ex-jailbirds and unemployed or unemployable hang out. Their home is a shopfront after it has closed for the day, a park bench, broken-down car or the pavement. Here is where the pawnshops abound, together with dingy, greasy ham-and-egg diners, knock houses, dangerous grubby bars, half-star flop houses rented by the hour and girlie bars.

You don't see tourists around here. The evil smell exuded by tiny X-rated movie houses, out-of-tune buskers and garbage is quite a contrast to fashionable Nob Hill — only a mile away. It is all underscored by the frequent wailing of police sirens.

71. Lennie

Walking through the terminal on the way down to the aircraft, I was approached by a rough-looking fellow who asked if I was on the flight to Hong Kong, working in Economy.

'Yes,' I replied, wondering what little problem was coming next. He surprised me by saying that Lennie (no surnames, no pack drill) was on the flight and he gave me $20 to look after him. Lennie was a well-known gangster. No problem. I found out which seat he was in and proceeded to give him the royal treatment — first-class wine and liqueur. About an hour into the flight, the passenger commented on how great the service was.

'But why are you calling me Lennie?'

'What?'

I raced up the front and looked again at the seating plan. Bum! S*#t! I've got the wrong seat.

I doubled the service to Lennie, and when we arrived in Hong Kong, as Lennie got off, he stopped and thanked me. He gave me his business card, saying, 'Get into any trouble, Brian, give me a call.' I found him to be a very nice man.

72. Warts and All

My friends all think I have a glamorous job: meeting and serving celebrities, the rich and famous, royalty, heads of state and, of course, happy passengers on holidays. Not so! It's like having the entire population of a small town on board — warts and all.

People getting drunk and then abusive, violent, demanding, timid; some falling in love, out of love, making love. Some are extroverts, others returning home injured after accidents, sometimes there are corpses in the hold; pregnant women; sick people; convicted felons being transported to jail; deportees and mentally disturbed people; and, of course, 'would-be-if-they-could-be' snobs.

73. Lunch with the Royals

Winter had arrived early in England with a vengeance, accompanied by sleet, snow, ice and fog. It was causing the usual havoc of delays and diversions to other airports.

We circled around Heathrow Airport for half an hour, burning fuel and adding to the already poor visibility. Then the port wing dropped and we diverted to Manchester Airport to wait for the fog to clear.

Manchester was as clear as a bell, shining in the early morning as we touched down and taxied around to the almost deserted terminal building.

Mr and Mrs Ponsonby in first-class were carrying on a right old treat. There went the call bell in first-class again.

'Yes Mrs Ponsonby, can I help you?' I enquired.

'Help me? Help me? How could you help me?' she snapped. 'Get the captain. I wish to speak to him about this inconvenient delay here in this dreadful Manchester.'

'He is busy right now, Mrs Ponsonby. There's nothing we can do until the fog lifts.'

'It's not good enough! My husband and I have a luncheon appointment at Windsor Castle. It's already 10am and, unless something starts happening real soon, we and somebody else will not be pleased.'

I was tempted to say, What do you expect us to do? Drive the 747 down the M1 freeway, you silly woman? We aren't doing this for fun.

Instead, I replied, 'Because we have not hung around like the other airlines, we are number one in the queue to take off for Heathrow.'

'It's not good enough,' she snapped, throwing up her gold-and-diamond-encrusted hand, demanding in a loud voice for all to hear, 'Isn't there another means of transport available we can use?' then adding, 'Money is no object — England has gone to the dogs.'

'I'll check for you, Madam.'

Our Manchester ground traffic officer was standing at the front door clutching a clipboard and had heard the commotion Mrs Ponsonby was kicking up.

Turning to me, he said, 'I'll bet you've had a lovely time with her all the way from Singapore.' With a grin, he continued, 'If you really want her off your hands, there is a charter helicopter here that does flights to London.'

'Try it, please.'

After a quick check on his two-way radio, he was back with the glad tidings that the helicopter pilot had checked the fog situation. It was quite clear at Windsor Castle. If we hurried, they could be on their way.

'Good news, Mrs Ponsonby,' I exclaimed in a loud voice for all who were tuned into this little incident with considerable interest.

'I've arranged for a helicopter to take you to the castle for only three hundred pounds. All we need is for you to come and clear immigration and customs. The pilot is getting permission to land on the castle grounds and you're away.'

'It doesn't matter now,' she hissed at me. 'Go away!'

There is a lesson to be learned here: Never stick your neck out if you might have to pull your head in. It was a very long, silent, one-hour flight back to Heathrow for the Ponsonbys, with the rest of first-class smirking. I felt pretty good too.

74. The lecture

During initial training to become a flight steward or air hostess years ago, there was a lecture on health and awareness while overseas; things like: don't eat salads, cold rice or fruits that were probably grown in (to put it bluntly) shit. Exercise and drink moderately (oh, yeah!) and don't smoke.

Then came the lecture on, Prevention is better than cure. Carol, a very pretty blonde nurse from the medical centre ran this course. Zap! The first picture was projected onto the screen a metre square, explicitly showing the effects of venereal disease (VD) on an organ. Yes — an organ, and not a musical instrument. Then another of gonorrhoea and another of syphilis! It certainly had us sitting upright! It reminded me when I was a young school boy looking at the pictures in the toilets on the railway station at Kingsgrove, with the word WARNING in large red letters, which terrified me (how do you get it?).

After the lecture and many pictures, as nurse Carol was opening the door to leave, she paused, looked back at us sitting like stunned mullets and said, 'Just remember boys, if she's fast and loose, there's a good chance she's got it — and if she's got it, you're gunna get it,' and slammed the door behind her.

I could hear her laughing outside. This lecture was

short-lived and was discontinued as being just a bit too strong and over the top. I was one of the 'privileged' few to have seen it before it got the chop. It truly was awful.

75. Head Gear and Ear Muffs

I witnessed an amazing number of silly things passengers did during flights, which we referred to as 'altitude antics' — but I think the person who wins the prize was a woman seated in the first-class cabin.

I was leaning on the first-class bar one sunny afternoon, having just finished the afternoon tea service, and I nonchalantly watched as Mrs ... well, let's call her 'Smith' (no name, no pack drill), an elderly passenger seated in 2B, casually stand up, kick off her shoes, then reach up under her dress. She pulled down her pink knickers and thrust them firmly down over the head of the businessman directly in front of her, who was reading the paper.

She then sat back down as if nothing had happened. The poor man leapt out of the seat with one eye peering out of a leg hole. Standing in the middle of the cabin, he yanked the mystery article off his head. He suddenly realised, with a confused look, that he was holding a pair of ladies' frilly scanties — and went berserk.

Mrs 'Smith', meanwhile, serenely sat there as if they weren't hers.

The embarrassed man headed for the toilet, thrusting the panties into the bar rubbish bin as he passed. He was in there a long, long time, cleaning himself up.

When confronted by the captain, Mrs 'Smith' denied any knowledge of it and, short of asking to see if she was wearing undies, there was nothing we could do about it.

'Please accept a couple of bottles of French champagne as a peace offering after this truly humiliating experience,' the captain said, trying hard not to smile at the man.

'A new Ferrari would not calm him down,' I murmured to myself, 'and you can't blame him.'

We never got to the bottom (no pun intended) of why she did it. That mortified man spent the rest of the flight nervously wondering what next could be coming over from behind. Perhaps her bra as ear muffs?!

76. Gamblers

Years ago, the crews seemed to be full of gamblers. Upon reaching a port after a hard flight, half the cabin crew would stay up most of the night gambling. More than once I saw the family car at home change hands. The wife would arrive at the airport to pick up the husband and find him asking for the keys. You can imagine the climate in the taxi on the way home.

One night in the old Cathay Hotel, which we called 'Cockroach Castle', in a big game it came down to the turn of a card, and the other player was questioned as to whether he had the money. The player jumped on the phone to the manager of his bank in Sydney to verify he did. It was 3:30 am. He lost.

The living-away allowances for a trip up to twenty-six days were originally given to crew members in Sydney for food (accommodation was paid for by the company). This had to be changed, as some of the crew members were gambling it away at the first port of call. It was then given to all crew at each port, which really didn't make much difference after all.

77. Jim

It was widely known that, if you were getting off at a transit port for any reason, you had to tell the chief steward so you were not left behind.

Jim was on his second trip in the company as supernumerary crew and nobody told him of this rule. He decided to have a look for a souvenir at the Manila airport. He didn't tell me.

Passengers re-boarded; we were cleared to go. I shut the door. Nobody missed Jim as he was an extra, and we were away taxiing down to the end for take-off.

I was in the flight deck giving the report: 'All fast forward aft, ship's papers on board, emergency drill completed, doors armed, 119 passengers on board and—'

The captain cut me off. 'Who's that running across the field?'

'It's Jim, our supernumerary crewman,' I groaned.

'What's he doing waving a handbag?' the captain asked.

'He must have bought it.'

The aircraft stopped on the taxiway, the engineer opened the hatch at his feet and Jim clambered on board. He had cut across through the marshes to catch us and was splattered with mud and stagnant water. He smelled like a sewer.

'Get him down the back and clean him up,' the captain hissed at me. 'I'll see you after take-off.'

Six weeks later at Auckland International, I closed the door prior to taxiing when I heard a loud thumping on the door.

I peered out through the small window set in the door, and standing there was the same annoyed captain.

78. Caught with my pants down

On long-haul, fourteen-hour flights, I did something that crews thought a bit strange. About half-way into the flight, I would go into the toilet, have a sponge wash and change my underwear, shirt and socks for fresh ones, and it was amazing how much better I felt.

A London basing was offered for eighteen months and I was one of the crew chosen to go with my family. On arrival in England, we were required to find our own accommodation for which the airline would pay. My family opted to live in the country and we found a small, picturesque village called Tetsworth on the Oxford Road, which was a two-hour drive to the airport. On my way to work, I did my little trick of driving down in civilian clothes and changing in the car park.

It was a cold, miserable day in December, with a heavy, swirling fog, as I drove into the nearly deserted car park, stopping next to a van for cover from the street. I hung my uniform on the roof-rack of the van and proceeded to take off my trousers, then turned to see that same van disappearing into the dense fog.

What to do? On the back seat were my Bermuda jacket and the pants I had just taken off. They were grey, so I went to work in them. I would worry about the uniform later.

As I stood at the door about to greet passengers, the traffic officer informed me that three of the Qantas board of directors were coming on the flight. Great! As luck would have it, the airline was trying out several styles of new uniform, and one of the directors, thinking I was wearing one, told me how modern and refreshing it was!

79. Captain Crap

Years ago, there was a captain who had a strange surname. His name was Captain Crap. A more likeable man would be hard to find, and he had a great sense of humour.

Julie was new to the crew on her second flight, and still very nervous when it came to making announcements over the intercom.

'Welcome aboard,' Julie announced in a chirpy voice. 'On behalf of Captain Crew and his crap we hope you have—' She stopped short, staring at me bent over laughing, and still holding the microphone button down, asked, 'Is his name really Crap?'

Out in the cabin, the passengers were in stitches laughing, and when I poked my head into the cockpit, there was the captain bent over the controls, guffawing too. It took some time to coax Julie out into the cabin, and longer for her to face the captain.

80. Ports

When I started flying in the early 1960s, we didn't have the new-fangled, flash suitcases now being used, with handles that extend, combination locks, waterproofing, wheels, and almost bulletproof — we had 'ports'. In old photos people had ports, with a tartan travel rug strapped to the side and the brolly slid along the side under the strap.

My first port was made out of compressed cardboard with elaborate hinges you could expand. Being a 'professional traveller' now, it lasted about three months. My next port was from Hong Kong and made of plywood, covered in fake black leather — it lasted six months. Taking note of what the old hands were using, I bought a Globite and it lasted ten years. My last port was a two-suiter Samsonite which lasted fifteen years of being tossed or kicked out of holds and onto conveyor belts. I still have it.

Frank (my old mate of the lady-stuck-in-the-toilet incident) and I were in Kowloon, Hong Kong, when he saw a flash, you-beauty suitcase in a store window. After the usual barter, he bought it and carried it back to the hotel, complaining all the way that maybe it was not a good choice as it was so heavy. When he opened it back in the hotel, there inside was another suitcase, and when he opened that, there was yet another one. I'll let you guess what Frank did about it!

Author with Skippy Squadron flag

Author and jet engine

My 1928 Ford five chief speedster

Skippy Squadron guys who did troop charters into Saigon Vietnam during the war

Skippy Squadron with Keith Payne VC

Speaking to Marie Bashir

The Author

The Flying Learys — Suzanne, me, Bart and Angela

This is your life with Jye and Zion Mitchell, both cardboard box babies

Zion Mitchell and me

81. Brains in your Suitcase

When I joined Qantas in 1962, interviews for the position of cabin crew were simple, uncomplicated affairs. 'Tell us about yourself,' they would ask, and look you up and down for neatness, reasonable looks, and half a brain. If they approved, you were in. Very different now, and very difficult to be selected.

At about the same time, a beautiful fashion model applied for the position. She was absolutely perfect in every way, and of course was selected to become a 'hostie." The selection committee was beaming, but as she got up to leave, she looked each of them in the eye and flippantly said, 'Anyway, passengers pack their brains in their suitcases before they go.' She didn't get the job.

After thirty years observing passengers, I think in some instances she was right, considering some of the incredible things they did. The majority of people, however, were great. But there seemed to be one or two on every flight who were real 'wallies'.

It never ceased to astonish me how people would travel all the way to Australia — and it is a bloody long way no matter where you come from — and not do any research whatsoever: how big our country is, its cultures, customs, and particularly our animals, so unique to us.

I could give you dozens of examples, but let's settle for one. While I was standing in the galley after the meal service reading the paper, I was startled when the galley curtain was thrust back and in walked a well-dressed, middle-aged man.

'Can I have a cup of coffee?' he asked.

'Sure, I'll make you one. Milk? Sugar?'

He was looking intently at my uniform jacket.

'What's that?' he asked, pointing at the breast pocket on my uniform coat.

I looked down and said patiently, 'It's a kangaroo, sir, which is the airline's trade mark.'

'No, no,' he insisted, 'that ...' pointing more closely.

'That's the wing on the kangaroo,' I replied.

With a stunned look, he said, 'Are you telling me, buddy, that not only do they hop, they fly?'

People never cease to amaze me.

82. It Takes All Types

Drinks were being served in the first-class cabin prior to departure on the trip to Djakarta. I was carefully easing the cork out of a chilled bottle of French champagne with a soft pop, when the well-dressed lady seated in Business, started making frantic signs, which caught my attention.

What now? I wondered. She's forgotten to turn the gas off at home — she's left her lipstick in the terminal toilet — or she wants the captain to ring her husband in Djakarta to meet her on arrival. These were just some of the many things I was asked to fix during my flying career.

'Yes, madam? Can I help you?'

'Steward,' she said in a hoity-toity voice, pointing a finger heavy with what looked like part of the Crown jewels towards the toilet. 'There are some frightfully ghastly sounds coming from inside there. Do something.'

'You are right, madam,' I said. 'I can hear it from here.' I was galvanised into action.

Toilets on the aircraft are designed so that, in an emergency such as this, by pulling down on a couple of catches, the door is released, allowing it to swing outwards. Little did I know just what I was in for. I pulled the catches.

It still chills me to recall the sight as the door swung out. He was middle-aged, tall and thin with receding hair. He was standing wide-eyed inside, covered in his own blood. My eyes flew to the basin — a nightmare sea of red, as were the walls and floor. Blood was running in lines down the mirror and dripping onto the stainless-steel bench as I stood transfixed in horror. The poor man took a single step towards me, then buckled at the knees, collapsing at my feet.

'Is there a doctor aboard?' I shouted loudly.

Almost immediately, a man appeared at my elbow, murmuring, 'You require a doctor, Steward?'

I stepped sideways to allow him to see the crumpled, blood-stained man on the floor.

'My god!' the doctor exclaimed fervently.

Here we go, I thought. Past experience had produced doctors of all kinds. Doctors of the arts, science, Egyptology and so on. But Dr Erickson was a medical practitioner.

My shouted call also alerted Lance and Eddie, two other stewards working in the cabin. They dropped what they were doing and hurried to help.

'Good Lord!' Our medical briefings didn't cover this kind of situation. Dishing out a few headache or airsick pills, the odd Band-Aid on a cut, plus knowing how to do CPR, was about it.

'You will be confronted occasionally with the unexpected,' my instructor from the school had said.

A quick examination by the doctor proved this was very serious.

'He needs a blood transfusion immediately. Can you organise it?' he calmly asked.

'You can bet I'll give it my best try,' I answered, sprinting up the stairs two at a time to the flight deck.

'Captain, get through to the airport medical centre. We need to give a transfusion to a passenger as soon as possible.'

Down the stairs again. It was obvious that time was fast running out for the wretched man. In the short time I was away he had deteriorated badly.

'Blood's on the way, Doctor,' I panted, staring at the poor fellow.

He was appealing to us with his eyes to help him, when, quite suddenly, he — just died.

The doctor stood up slowly and said, 'He didn't have a chance, I'm afraid.' Looking at us, he added, 'Are you fellas alright?'

Lance, Eddie and I just stood there in a state of shock. Was it only two or three minutes ago I was quietly serving champagne in first-class, humming a tune to myself? We didn't even know his name.

More trauma was thrust on us when the ground personnel refused to remove the body from the aircraft. Being already spattered with his blood, it fell upon us to carry the poor man past the seated passengers, down to the van now waiting at the bottom of the steps. Ground crew supplied other uniforms for us to wear for the flight because there was no slackening or counselling in those days.

Next morning, Lance told me he had spent most of the night weeping and in shock after seeing the man's ghastly death. Eddie also had spent the night in turmoil. Me? I showered, changed into clean clothes, found the nearest bar and put a dent in a bottle of rum.

On our return to Sydney, at debriefing we were informed that Mr Clinton had died from advanced tuberculosis, splitting his lung after apparently going into a coughing fit.

Months went by, then I ran into Lance in Oxford Street, London. Standing by the busy road, the horrific ordeal all came back. Over a drink in the 'Bunch of Grapes', Lance told me he had just come off sick pay since the death and was still getting treatment. He told me he had great difficulty eating or drinking anything red. Eddie caught a mild form of tuberculosis and also spent some time off on sick pay. Me? When signing on for my next flight, I was called into the office. The manager explained that they had received a letter from a gentleman who was seated near where the tragic incident occurred and had observed the whole thing.

Hello, I thought to myself. For once I'm going to be congratulated for what we had done and gone through. Maybe, I thought, they are going to recognise my efforts by giving my wife and me a free ticket to Hong Kong or Hawaii. Alas, no. The gentleman complained bitterly in his letter how he had saved for some time for the airfare and was demanding another, free, ticket because, 'Chief Steward Leary spoilt my trip by not smiling once all the way to Djakarta.'

'You will meet all types,' George had said. How right he was.

83. Fence Wire and UFOs

It is often said that you have to be mad to fly as a job. Most of us had a fatalistic attitude to the whole business, and the ones who worried or had premonitions about flying didn't last very long. They would go sick if they thought something may happen or go wrong. We were quite often asked by passengers if we were scared of flying? Our standard answer was, 'No, but I'm scared of dying.'

The word 'crash' was a no-no word in the 'good old days' among crew, and was rarely mentioned or spoken about. Indeed, up until the Jumbo 747s arrived, if there happened to be an airline crash somewhere, newspapers were not loaded on board for that day. I've often wondered why they changed this attitude as it was a very nice gesture. We have all had a near miss or two in the family car, so why should it be different in the plane?

The night in question was at the old Singapore airport in the early 1960s (the runway is now part of the highway going into the city). We were thundering merrily down the runway in the Super Constellation, the Merlin engines purring away as the propellers made their particular flapping sound. During take-off, lots of cabin crew, including me, counted to themselves: one, two, three. Between around twenty-six and thirty-two, depending on the passenger load, you were usually airborne. Bloody hell! I was up to forty-four!

Bucking and bouncing, we tore down the strip, zooming over the perimeter fence, picking up the top strand of wire with the undercarriage. Twang! The captain was fighting the controls to make more height as we carried on so low that we could see people having dinner in the shanties bordering the airfield. It must have scared the hell out of them as well, as we howled on by.

About a kilometre out, we struggled to a height where a 180-degree turn could be made, and landed heavily back on the same runway we had just left. It must have been one of the shortest flights of an international aircraft on record. That night, the captain bought drinks all round in the bar, informing us, as he held up his hand with the index finger and thumb about two inches apart, that we had been that close to making it onto the back page of the newspaper (obituaries).

An inspection of the aircraft revealed that some idiot from the cargo section had shoe-horned a heavy piece of machinery into the front hold. It had, of course, thrown the aircraft completely out of trim, giving us very little lift, which was the reason we just made it over the fence.

*

Years ago, a ship used as a navigational aid called 'Checkboat Charlie' was moored permanently halfway between San Francisco and Honolulu in the Pacific Ocean. In the 1960s we didn't have the sophisticated, computerised systems of today that finally made 'Charlie' obsolete. Navigators are no longer required to peer through a periscope to sight a fix by the stars and have, alas, joined Charlie in the history books, like radio officers before them. Who's next? The pilots?

We were approaching the halfway mark and point-of-no-return when the lights first appeared. The cockpit was softly lit by the red glow of the instrument panel, the technical crew had all eaten, were relaxed and looking out through the windscreen.

'What's that?' asked the captain, sitting upright and pointing out through the triple-laminated windscreen. A row of bright lights had appeared quite suddenly, directly in our flight path and travelling in the same direction. Looking swiftly on the green-lit radar screen hypnotically going around showed nothing.

'Good Lord, it's only about a thousand metres ahead on the same flight plan,' the first officer exclaimed as the captain took evasive action.

Time slipped by with the mysterious lights still keeping pace ahead of our aircraft, the technical crew at a loss to know what it could be. It then started to drift about, first to port, then starboard, always keeping the same distance away.

'Maybe it is reflected light from the moon,' the second officer suggested.

'Reflected on what?' snapped the captain. 'It's as clear as crystal and there's no cloud.'

'Charlie' came up underneath and the captain called them up, asking if they could see the puzzling lights.

'No,' came the reply from the ship. 'We can see you clearly in the night sky, but there are no lights in front of you.'

'That's settled it,' the captain announced. 'I'm calling up the USA Airforce Base in Honolulu.'

The USAF jet fighter arrived about a half hour later and flew close in alongside us, off the starboard wing.

'Where are these mysterious lights that's bothering you?' asked the fighter pilot in a slow Texan drawl.

'There, there, right in front of us,' replied the captain, pointing ahead. The jet fighter stayed with us all the way to Honolulu but did not even get a glimpse of the lights we could all see so clearly for more than two hours. Just before descent into Honolulu, the lights blinked several times, then accelerated at incredible speed and were gone.

It was written up in the records as 'mysterious lights of unknown origin' by the authorities in Hawaii. To me, though, they will always be UFOs.

84. Hotels We Stayed In

Years ago, 'in the good old days', crew were treated as valued employees — not like now when they seem to be considered expendable workhorses. Experience does not seem to count anymore either. Our accommodation, I must say, where available, was mostly superb. But in some of the second- and third-world countries it was basic and, at times, absolutely dreadful.

Even so, at the annual crew reunions, mention some of the dreadful ones and crews' eyes light up. Nobody is going to get too excited if you mention the St Moritz in New York City right on Central Park; the Fairmont on Nob Hill in San Francisco; the Marunouchi Japanese-style hotel in Tokyo; the Mayfair in London; the Gulf in Bahrain; or the Sheraton in Hong Kong Harbour. These were all places that we stayed in over the years.

Then there were places like Speedbird House in Karachi, Pakistan, which after we left was turned into a prison. Crews ran riot day and night there. The Intercontinental Hotel in Tehran was another gem. It had been converted into a hotel from being the general hospital. The crew-room was in the basement, which was previously the morgue, complete with the stainless-steel doors in the wall. The foyer had a huge Persian carpet on the floor. On closer inspection (the last time I was there) there were six carpets, placed one on top of the other as they wore out.

The Nile Hilton in Cairo had a novel solution for when the hotel was full or overbooked — simple. They put crews in their floating houseboats, moored up against the private hotel wharf. It was great.

The La Sharland Hotel in Mauritius was situated

right on the beach front — and 200 metres up the beach was the hospital where the nurses were billeted. Very convenient for some of the stewards. The manager cared little about rules and regulations. In fact, he cared little about anything. Some of the parties there are still regarded as legendary.

The hotel in Zimbabwe had an arrangement where you could transfer to the Whange Safari Park an hour away and stay in the tree houses.

Years ago in Singapore, before they ruined it with high-rise monstrosities, we stayed at the Colonial Park Hotel by the water's edge. It was straight out of the 1920s with ceiling fans, pot plants, shutters, cane chairs, palms, fountains and turbaned waiters. Sydney Greenstreet and Humphrey Bogart would have been quite at home there. It's gone now, replaced with yet another block of flats.

Our original accommodation in Bali was in a very old hotel with the swimming pool encircling the building. It didn't stop it burning down!

We all hated the hotel in Manchester, England, which had the dubious honour of having the smallest hotel rooms (I suspect) in the world. They were made even smaller because a massive wardrobe had been shoe-horned into each room. Knowing that we were only staying two days, not six months, was the only way we coped with it. To watch TV with any degree of comfort one had to sit in the hallway with the door open or get into bed.

The foyer in the Lexington Hotel in New York City was a fun place to sit and watch the rich and famous film stars, TV personalities and whores who walked by. In the Roaring Twenties, Al Capone occupied the penthouse. In an alcove on the outside of the hotel was the Chatter Box coffee shop, right on the footpath — another great place to watch the world go by. We stayed there many times over the years.

Nothing fancy about the Drake Wiltshire in San Francisco except that it was managed by Mary and Ben, who considered the Australian crews to be their family. They knew us all by name and were the nicest of people. Of course, there is always one. A steward borrowed money from Mary and never paid it back. He was blackballed by crews until the day he left the airline. Maybe that is why he left?

Big, rowdy, clumsy Sammy would always come running to greet a new busload of tourists or a crew booking into the Siam Intercontinental Hotel in Bangkok. It was a real treat to see him and to watch as the tourists, mouths open in amazement, saw an orphaned baby elephant charging at them. Yeah — he was the hotel pet, with free range of the palatial tropical gardens, and even the pool area and reception. It went on for years and then he was gone. Unfortunately for him, he grew into a bull elephant with tusks, and was knocking over tables by the pool where people were eating. He was also leaving steamy, smelly pats all over the place. He now resides at a safari park about 60 kms away. We missed Sammy.

85. Welcome Aboard

Initiation jokes were part-and-parcel of most jobs and airline crews were definitely no exception. They were expert at embarrassing the squeaky-clean poor wretch on a first flight.

The Australian government in the early 1970s was chartering Boeing aircraft and crews to fly to Athens, Greece, to transport plane-loads of Greeks to Australia as migrants. Our new hostie, Diane, on her very first flight and full of enthusiasm, was standing beside me at the front door of the aircraft waiting to greet the migrant passengers. Across the tarmac came a long line of Australia-bound future Aussies carrying baskets, boxes and babies, looking a little bewildered. Diane, noting the forlorn look on many of their faces as they prepared to leave their homeland, turned to me and asked, 'What should we say to them as a friendly greeting to cheer them up?'

Greg, the only Greek-speaking steward on the flight, known throughout the airline for his dry wit, was leaning casually against the door jamb, his hands thrust deep in his pockets. Watching the snaking column of people, he spontaneously answered, '*Shatatis Kota* will do them.'

Pushing himself off the door-frame, he sauntered down to the rear of the plane to pour fruit juices. Our enthusiastic new girl heard this remark and as the 130 migrants filed past her at the door, most of them with tears in their eyes, she brightly said *Shatatis Kota* to them all.

Diane didn't seem to notice the odd stares she was receiving in return for her warm welcome. After they were all seated and documentation was completed, we went about giving them a fruit juice, Diane bringing up the rear with cool towels in a wicker basket, now and again saying *Shatatis Kota*.

She returned to the galley to refill the basket with towels where Greg was busy pouring juices from a jug into plastic cups. Diane asked him, 'By the way, Greg, what does *Shatatis Kota* mean?'

Greg looked up and replied, 'Hey! You remembered what I said.'

'Yes, I did, and I said it to every passenger as they boarded,' she proudly stated.

The look on his face was priceless, the jug of juice poised over the cups.

'What?' he said incredulously. 'You just said 'chicken shit' to them all!'

*

It is amazing how many of the crew fancied themselves as would-be radio announcers, never missing an opportunity to use the public address system. This went on for years with crew members making stupid announcements about trivial things. Some even did it in the middle of the night, waking everybody up, until order was returned by making one person responsible for all announcements.

An example was the steward who, giving the hand basin and bench top in the toilet a clean-up, found a really expensive-looking diamond ring. Straight onto the PA system, he blurted out, 'Would the lady who lost her ring in the rear toilet please report immediately to the senior steward.'

It took a long time before the laughter died down and even longer for the poor lady to come and claim the ring.

A wallet, bulging with American one-hundred-dollar bills, was found lying on the floor in the aisle. The inevitable announcement was made, 'If the person who lost his wallet full of one-hundred-dollar bills would care to reclaim it, he can join the queue about to start at the forward door.'

If the plane was full, Sydney to London in Economy could be a real ordeal. Add a delay in Singapore and again in Bahrain and it became plain awful, with the passengers disembarking in London, sticky, sweaty and dog tired.

The passengers were filing off past me at the front door when along came a lady followed by her husband, looking dishevelled and carrying all manner of parcels. Little Johnny was bringing up the rear when, just as they got to me, the flow of passengers stopped. The little lad, not looking where he was going, bumped into his dad's behind, and then exclaimed in a loud voice, 'Hey Dad, your bum stinks!' How do you explain that to a planeload of strangers?

86. I quit, So Can You

Want to give up smoking? Fly to New York City!

It was a freezing winter day in January as I aimlessly wandered the streets of New York City, hunched up in my overcoat, rabbit fur cap and scarf. I was smoking a cigarette, cursing the roster clerk who put me on this trip. I was not to know that within a few minutes I was to make a decision that would save not only my health, but also my life.

I was on Fifth Avenue and passed Tiffany's jewellery store with snow spiralling all around. The store next door had an awning, so I sheltered under it until the snow eased off. It was the cancer clinic. There were two large display windows, one on each side of the doorway. Looking at the first display window, I saw that the whole inside was painted black, with a pair of lungs hanging down, lit by a single spotlight. A sign beneath revealed that the lungs were from a healthy farmer from Kansas, who had never smoked.

I moved over to the second display window and BAM! Same scene, this time with a pair of black lungs dripping with crap running down and onto the display floor. This time the sign said that it was also from a farmer, but that he'd smoked twenty cigarettes a day for twenty years. Next to this window was a very large bin, filled to the brim with the scrunched-up cigars and cigarettes of people who had seen the light. I screwed up mine; they joined the pile and I hurried back to the warmth of the hotel.

87. That's Hong Kong, Sir

It was summertime in steamy Hong Kong before it devolved into a modern city and lost all its character. In a 707 aircraft, we taxied around and parked out on the apron about forty metres from the old Kai Tak terminal.

I threw open the front door of the aircraft, breathing in the humid combination of smells. It was reminiscent of boiled rice, raw fish and a compost heap. There was a loud, nasal American voice behind me asking, 'Hey Steward, what the hell's that smell?'

Turning, I brightly said, 'That's Hong Kong, sir.' It's ironic that the Chinese characters for Hong Kong mean 'fragrant harbour'.

88. Connie and Harry

Connie was groaning. Connie was dying. Her temperature was escalating rapidly to well over 100oF (37.8C). The skin was being literally stripped from her frame. Yeah, she was a goner.

The day was sunglasses weather at Madagascar airfield as passengers boarded the plane bound for Singapore, all in an 'ain't-we-lucky' mood. Clearance had been received. The plane trundled down the runway which had a dip in the end giving the illusion of it disappearing into the ground before it leapt skywards.

It was speeding up perfectly, the Pratt & Whitney engines purring. Senior Steward Harry was seated on the jump seat at the rear of the plane. He was gazing casually at the wall of sugar cane growing right up to the edge of the runway.

The aircraft had passed the point on the runway known as V2, which meant you were committed to go, no matter what. A series of backfires erupted from the starboard engine — the plane thundered on through the perimeter fence, laying it flat. Those magnificent five-foot propeller blades shredded the cane in the neighbouring field like hail before bursting through a dry-stone wall and ending up straddling a ditch.

Yeah! Connie was never going to spread her wings again. She was a legend among the air crew, that old

Super Constellation 1049.

Harry knew with a sinking feeling as it went through the fence that the time had come for him to earn his wages. Unclipping his seatbelt, he leapt across to the emergency door, automatically looking for fire outside before throwing it open.

A different sound erupted from inside the cabin as terrified, panic-stricken passengers descended on him, yelling and screaming and then baulking at jumping from this height into a ditch. Grabbing passengers by their collars and seats of their pants, Harry began launching passengers through the door like bags of wheat.

He stopped for a breather after ten or so passengers had been ejected in this manner and he glanced out the door to see how things were progressing. As serious as the situation was, Harry burst out laughing. All the passengers he had thrown out were still in the creek, piled high in a pyramid of arms and legs, covered in stinking mud.

Fate, the relentless hunter, was kind that day as everyone escaped, limping away. The local newspaper said it was a miracle no one perished as the aircraft was completely burned out. It went on to say, Just a few breaks and sprains. Mostly caused by Harry.

89. Soup Kitchen and Hank and Larry

As I have an interest in vintage cars and memorabilia, particularly car badges, I planned to spend the day at an auto-wrecking yard on the outskirts of San Francisco. I had gotten to know the owner and he let me roam around his yard, sometimes for hours. I dressed in my old working clothes that I had brought with me — you don't go to a wrecking yard in good clothes. I caught sight of my appearance in the bathroom mirror and decided to leave the fashionable Hilton Hotel, where we were staying, via the rear exits. Briskly, I crossed the road and strode around the corner.

A well-dressed guy in a windcheater stepped out of a doorway as, deep in thought, I walked past. He grabbed me by the arm, swinging me in full stride around, and propelling me through a doorway.

'What's going on?' I asked in a startled voice.

'Here you go, buddy,' the man replied with a smile, pressing a Hershey candy bar, a pack of smokes and book of matches into my hand. I blinked and looked about to see the place was some kind of a church hall, crowded with down-on-their-luck, depressed-looking men. They were all seated at trestle tables slurping steaming bowls of thick soup. I was in a soup kitchen for the homeless!

'Wait, I'm not—' I started to say.

The man cut me off, saying quietly, 'Come on, friend. Don't be ashamed. Enjoy a bowl of soup.'

Not wanting to cause a fuss or any embarrassment, and observing at the same time how impeccably clean the place was — I did. A man sat across the table from me dressed in an old stained army coat. I judged him to be roughly my own age. Under the table was a scruffy little dog that the man was feeding the chunky bits of the soup.

Pushing my chocolate bar and smokes across, with a nod I said, 'My name is Brian. Here take these, I don't smoke.'

'Thanks,' he said. 'Call me Hank and,' pointing with his spoon, 'that's Larry under the table.' He fell silent until I got up to leave, when he surprised me by saying, 'God bless you.'

I stopped to thank the doorman and he handed me another candy bar, saying, 'Come again, friend.'

That night, flying at 38,000 feet on the way to Honolulu, serving caviar, lobster mornay and chocolate gateau to the first-class passengers, I thought about it all and wondered, *Who would have been more embarrassed if the doorman happened to have been one of the passengers I was serving?*

San Francisco was a regular port of call for me. Passing Macy's Department Store one evening, I saw a man wearing an army overcoat crawling into a cardboard box for the night as he called to a little dog piddling on a fire hydrant. It was Hank and Larry. Each time I visited the City by the Bay after that, I always detoured around by Macy's, visiting Hank and Larry, bringing a hamburger for each of them. Hank never asked for anything in all the time I knew him — he wasn't a bum; he just chose to live that way.

The Franciscan Cathedral is a beautiful structure built with sandstone blocks in the traditional fashion of arches, columns, towers and flying buttresses. Nowadays its official name is The National Shrine of Saint Francis of Assisi. It is situated behind the hotel where we stayed in the now-unfashionable part of town, down by Market Street.

One Sunday morning during Mass, the collection plate was doing the rounds of the seated parishioners, when the person beside me handed it to me. I absently put money on it and handed it to the church warden standing in the aisle. It was Hank. With a wink he took it and moved on. As I left the church after the service, there — tied to the iron railing out the front — was Larry, madly wagging his tail at me.

90. Race Day

The hotel we stayed in at Kuala Lumpur, Malaysia, during the 1980s fronted onto the magnificent horse-racing track renowned for its impeccable gardens.

It was Saturday morning and I had been woken by the sound of a crowd cheering and loudspeakers blaring.

'What the hell's that?' I muttered, throwing back the curtains.

'Stunning' would be an understatement.

I had a box-seat view of the whole track laid out before me: magnificent lawns, gardens in full bloom, sparkling fountains and an immaculately manicured green turf track.

Grandstands on the opposite side of the track were crowded with punters shouting and waving their arms, while the loudspeakers provided the commentary.

'You little beauty,' I exclaimed.

As I stared, I realised something was very much amiss. Where were the thoroughbreds, where were the colourfully clad jockeys? A quick phone call to hotel reception soon put me right.

'There are no actual races here in KL, sir,' the receptionist informed me. 'All races are broadcast direct from the track in Singapore — but you can go and bet with the bookies,' she said.

What a disappointment! No, I didn't go. I wonder if they have real races now?

91. Crews

Crews during the 'golden years' of flying, 1958–1972, were a family. We all knew one another — where we all lived, our families and even our pets. We also looked after each other — except for the bludgers, dobbers, smarties, and those who took advantage of others. For instance, there was a delightful girl flying who was great to work with. But she came down with rheumatoid arthritis. She struggled on for some time with the help of crews. She once told me she had to put her own call-time in at hotels one hour earlier as it took her that long to get ready. Nobody told the company and eventually she had no choice but to resign. 'Mum's the word'.

On the other side of the coin, there was a girl who had a nice little rort going — until I stopped it. The busiest time on a long trip was always straight after take-off out of Sydney. Passengers had to find their way to the airport, usually without a decent meal, then be faced with queues for booking, immigration, security, delays, excess baggage, tearful departures ... compassionate grounds the reasons were endless. So, after take-off, they all wanted a drink, food, pens, playing cards and so on.

The girl in question always put on her tearful little act, that she had had a fight with her boyfriend and could not work until she composed herself. Supervisory crew fell for this every time, putting her in the crew-rest until she recovered, while the rest of the crew, suddenly one short, struggled on doing the service. I was on a flight when she pulled this little caper, and I asked the guy working with me how he felt about leaving home. He said his family were all down with the 'flu' and he didn't want to go either.

Right. We both joined the girl still sobbing away in the crew-rest, putting our feet up, reading the papers. It wasn't long before we were asked what the hell we were doing. We answered, 'We move when she does.'

The word was out about her; crew-rooms were talking and saying they had experienced this with her, too. She didn't last long after that and she left without the usual farewell party.

I've been told that these days, a whole trip to England and back can be done without some of the crew members even introducing themselves to one another.

When I retired, the crew presented me with one of the wheel chocks on arrival at home base for the last time. I treasure it and use it for a door stop.

92. The Gourmet Breakfast

The flight to Honolulu left Sydney every day at 7pm, or 1900 hours in aeronautical terms, with drinks being served soon after take-off, followed by dinner. Prior to landing in Honolulu, nine hours later, a full breakfast was also served. Tony, a bundle of nerves, was on his first flight and had been delegated to work the rear galley, heating up the 300 or so economy-class and thirty-eight business-class meals. I was just about to start the first-class dinner, which is cooked in the galley up front, when Tony appeared at my elbow.

'Could I have a word with you, chief?' he whispered nervously.

'Yes, what's up, Tony?' I enquired, placing more wine glasses on the trolley.

'I've cooked the business-class breakfasts instead of the dinners, that's what's up,' he replied in dismay, wringing his hands.

'Let's have a look at them.' I sighed as I headed down the back, knowing from past experience that the omelettes, once they were heated, had to be served immediately or they turned green.

Yes, as I predicted, when I pulled the rack out of the oven, there were thirty-eight, emerald-green omelettes staring back at me.

'Pity we have not got an Irish convention on board,' I said, trying to make light of the situation. 'Chuck them out. Get the dinner meals heated up real quick and we'll see what we can do about it later,' I ordered.

After the dinner was finished, I went around to all the crew, including the pilot, telling them the sad story. They all had to admit that they had made a few mistakes in their time, and donated their crew meal towards the business-class breakfast. Only one would not give up his meal. There's always one.

'Right, Tony,' I said, rubbing my hands together. 'We have eighteen meals and here's how we are going to make them thirty-eight.'

Turning to my cook, I said, 'Bob, we will start our first-class breakfast thirty minutes early. Cook up everything you have.'

As soon as the last first-class passenger had his main course, we loaded up the tray-mobile with all the food not served, plus the crew meals. It worked.

Several weeks passed by and then a note from the crew manager was placed in my file. It said that four business-class passengers on that flight had written in commending the airline on upgrading the meals and giving them a bit of interest.

The menu that day read: steak, fish, chicken, mixed grill, lasagne, beef stroganoff, pancakes, scrambled eggs, bacon, tomatoes, mushrooms and hash browns. I'd say that was a bit better than emerald-green omelettes! I didn't tell the manager why. Tony-muck-up-the-meals hasn't forgotten, either.

93. Bolt Upright

Situated on the left inside the front door of the old Mauritius Airport was the duty-free shop. Because time was limited for us to prepare the aircraft for the next sector, the duty-free store managers kindly gave us priority over passengers in purchasing our liquor.

We were busily ordering our supplies one trip when a Japanese gentleman stepped up to the counter, dressed immaculately in a bowler hat, pin-stripe suit and carrying an expensive-looking briefcase. In no time he became very irritable at having to wait, particularly behind crew. Turning to me in faltering English, he said, 'I first-class. I go before you.' The steward standing next to me, who was a real smart-aleck, heard this and replied in the same faltering way, 'Nip off, Nippon,' bowing from the waist.

The Japanese man was highly insulted at this remark and, before I could make any amends to him, he stormed off into the crowded terminal.

'You stupid bastard, Cliff. One of these days you'll get us into real trouble with that smart-arse talk. Wake up to yourself,' I said, glaring at him.

Just as we were about to leave, the Japanese man came striding back and he had the airline station manager with him. The station manager was a likeable, easy-going fellow whom I knew quite well. He told me we were in deep shit, as the man beside him was a director of one of the largest corporations in Japan, and he wanted all our names. Turning to Cliff, I said, 'Well, my prophesy didn't take very long to come true, did it?' There was no way I was giving him my name and I was frantically trying to think of a way out of this mess.

With his solid-gold pen, the Japanese man pointed at me, being the chief steward and most senior crew member, saying, 'Name, please.'

'Bolt Upright,' I spontaneously replied. The Japanese man meticulously wrote this into his notebook. It looked like the station manager was going to explode — he couldn't look at me for fear of laughing.

'You next,' the gentleman with the gold pen demanded, looking narrowly at Cliff.

'Victor Mower,' Cliff replied without any further remarks, *thank goodness*.

Rhonda, the hostess, was next, and was quick to catch onto our act, announcing, 'My name is Rounda Bend.'

Frank, my old mate from the pea-soup and lady-stuck-in-the-toilet incidents, was shaking his head at me as if to say, 'Another fine mess you've gotten me into, Brian.'

'Rick Shaw,' Frank answered, looking the Japanese in the eye. *Four down and two to go*, I thought to myself, hoping the last two would come up with something.

'I've done nothing wrong,' the second-last steward said, 'but if you want my name, it's Luke Warm.' It was duly recorded in the little black book.

The last crew member was on his first trip and determined not to be left holding the bag was written all over his face. 'Nil Deposit,' he simply said in a strong voice. I liked that answer as his first name was Nyall. *He'll be okay flying*, I thought.

On board the plane, I was still berating Cliff as passengers started to board, when who should appear at the door but the Japanese director.

'Struth! He's one of our first-class passengers! It was not an easy flight home to Sydney as nothing was good enough according to the executive. He gave us all a terrible time and we were never so happy to get off a flight. Strangely, we never heard a word about it, and can only conclude that when he wrote his formal complaint, the office must have thought it was someone having a joke with them.

94. Room 1306

The Ilikai Hotel was a favourite place for our crews slipping into Honolulu and had been for the best part of twenty years. It was situated right on the ocean front with beautiful views looking out to sea, red sunsets and Diamond Head in the distance. There were comfortable, big rooms, a separate lounge and even a fully equipped kitchen for those who chose to do a spot of cooking.

The ocean-front rooms all had odd numbers such as 1805, and the street-side ones were even-numbered. Crews were supposed to get the cheaper street-side rooms but now and then we got lucky and enjoyed the extra luxuries of the sunny, ocean-front rooms.

I took note of the times that the hotel clerk chose to give me one of these super-duper rooms, and wouldn't you know it, it was always on the thirteenth floor. Hmm.

Speaking of the thirteenth floor, room number 1306 on the street-side had a little secret that the hotel didn't know about. The New Zealand and Australian crews sure did. You see, behind the large, framed abstract picture of the setting sun on the wall over the divan, somebody always puts the latest Playboy and Penthouse magazines after having read them. Of course, with the number of times I was flying in and out of Hawaii, I knew my chances were very good of eventually getting 1306 and checking out the secret.

'Mr Leary, Room 1306.' The female receptionist, smiling sweetly, added, 'Have a fun time,' slamming the key down on the marble-top counter.

Murmuring, 'Thank you,' I wondered if it was such a well-kept secret after all! Several crews made remarks like, 'Can I have the mags after you, Brian?' and 'I guess we won't be seeing you for the rest of the day.'

Was it my imagination, or did the lift always stop short by about fifty millimetres on the thirteenth floor? Who cares? Bumping my Samsonite suitcase over the lip of the lift floor, I headed down towards 1306. As I flung the case onto the luggage stand, I contemplated whether to have a shower first or look to see what was behind Pandora's picture. Reaching behind the frame, I said to myself, Ha ha, there IS something there. I pulled it out with a flourish and with eyes like organ stops. I realised I was holding a two-day-old copy of a daily newspaper from Sydney.

95. Fun Flights

Fun flights were introduced by the airlines in the 1970s to boost holiday sales to the South Pacific islands. To add to the gaiety, we were issued with batik-patterned beach shirts which were anything but fun to wear, made out of coarse material and hot as hell. Some bright spark in the office also suggested we could have horse-racing games on board. They were broadcast over the PA and were of the previous Saturday's Sydney races while the video caught the action on the screens throughout the cabin. It was a huge success with old ladies who had probably never been on a plane, or to a race meeting, yelling 'Go, go!' Punters were having side bets with one another and there were arguments over photo finishes.

All the winners were given bottles of champagne to take off the aircraft and drink on their holiday. One of the young stewards would occasionally conceal a winning ticket on the bottom of the pile he was giving out until he came to a charming young lass travelling alone. Like a riverboat gambler, he would deal it out from the bottom to her, murmuring with a smile, 'I hope you can win. Can I help you drink it in Fiji?'

Swaying palms on balmy nights with the water lapping on a sandy beach as the moon rose saw one or two fun-flight stewards sipping champers with pretty girls. A suggestion was also put to the company that we have blue denim flights with the seats and crew decked out in denim. I can only guess at what mischief crews would have gotten themselves into had it been introduced.

96. A Royal Hello

I seemed to have spent half my lifetime standing at the front door of an aircraft and there I was yet again, watching two traffic officers roll out a plush red carpet from the terminal to the bottom of the steps of the 707 at Nandi, Fiji's airport.

Hello, somebody important must be flying with us today and Management haven't bothered to inform the crew, I thought with irritation.

The army marched out smartly, lining up on both sides of the carpet and forming a guard of honour.

The police band struck up a marching tune as the VIP stepped out of the terminal.

'Good heavens,' I said, instantly recognising him. 'It's the ex-king of England, Edward VIII, who abdicated the throne in 1936.'

The look on his face said it all; how fed up he was with all the pomp and ceremony, looking neither left nor right. Wendy, the hostess standing beside me at the door had a sudden thought, saying to me in panic, 'What should we call him?'

'Leave it to me,' I answered, observing the way he was ignoring all the hoo-ha. He climbed the stairs to the aircraft door and silently stood there, expecting more bowing, scraping and saluting.

'How yer going, mate? Welcome aboard.'

Wendy almost collapsed. Edward looked intently at me in surprise and astonishment. A broad smile lit up his face as he replied, 'Good heavens! A human being!' Putting his hand on my shoulder, we walked together into the cabin where I showed him his seat. 'Please sit for a moment and chat with me,' he asked, his eyes twinkling at the unexpected greeting.

'Yes, by all means,' I replied.

If the former king of England, Ireland and the Colonies, Emperor of India, His Royal Highness the Duke of Windsor commands me to chat, I'm your man. When I think back now to this most pleasant human interaction, I'm surprised at the risk I took in addressing him that way even though I meant no disrespect.

What a charming gentleman. I very much doubt that he had ever before been addressed in such a manner.

97. Rorting Roy

The brass door knocker sounded knockedy knock, knock just as my wife and I were about to sit down to lunch at our home. Annette went to answer it.

'Good afternoon, madam,' a cheery voice said in a way that was familiar, but from where? 'Our company is doing a promotion in this area on electric light bulbs,' the voice continued. 'Did you know the average home has twenty bulbs? Our company, for the nominal fee of seven dollars, will change each and every bulb for you. The average life of a bulb is six months and—'

'G'day, Roy. I thought it was you. How's retirement treating you?' I interrupted, coming to the door. We had known each other for years in the crew ranks until Roy retired early on account of a badly broken leg, which he sustained in a car accident and it hadn't healed quite right.

'Oh hello, Brian,' Roy said, looking a little embarrassed and ill-at-ease. 'What's the promotion you have going on lightbulbs, mate?'

Roy was in retreat now.

'I don't think this is for you, old mate,' he said, starting to limp down the driveway.

I walked down with him to the small blue Ford van parked across the street. Nearing the van, a voice from inside asked. 'How many bulbs on this one, Dad?'

Sitting on an upturned milk crate in the back was Roy's son, hunched over a pail of soapy water, busily washing fly-spotted bulbs and polishing up the brass ends with steel wool. Roy was suddenly in a hell of a hurry to get away, mumbling as he got into the driver's seat, 'See you around.' He drove off, leaving behind a trail of smoke from the labouring engine and a stream of frothy water leaking out through the back doors from the overturned bucket.

Annette and I went back to our lunch wondering what it was all about, but knowing it was some sort of rort, and Roy now had his son on as an apprentice.

I was standing out the front next day watering the lawn when Jack, my next-door neighbour, put his head over the fence and asked, 'Did you take up the lightbulb offer yesterday, Brian?'

'No, I didn't.'

'We did. It seemed like a pretty good deal to us. Funny thing though, I had a look around after he had left and there were all sorts of brands. He must be representing quite a few of the bulb companies.'

The penny dropped! I knew Roy was onto something shifty. What he was doing was changing all the lightbulbs just as he promised and after a quick clean in the van was putting them in the next house.

The only person who probably got a fair deal was the first house he swindled because he would have needed bulbs to start with unless he did his own home first.

98. Room for Two

What am I doing walking around in this weather in Nagoya, Japan? It was like a blizzard, with the wind howling along the narrow street, swirling snow falling heavily, and it was bitterly cold. For the tenth time I asked myself, What are you doing out in this, you idiot?

I was beginning to look like Mr Frosty and not a taxi in sight. There wasn't even anywhere to shelter. The tiny houses on both sides of the street were tightly shuttered and closed up. Out of the white haze, a Japanese man appeared, appropriately dressed for blizzard conditions, sheltering under a large, strong umbrella. He came up level with me and glancing at the state I was in, said, 'Come, come. Share with me, there's room for two,' indicating the umbrella.

'Thank you,' I shouted above the noise of the wind-driven snow. We walked a block in silence huddled under the brolly when suddenly he grabbed my arm and steered me towards a Pachinko parlour. It was lit up like a Christmas tree with flickering lights running in relays across the front.

Pachinko is a popular game in Japan in which small buckets of steel ball-bearings are purchased from a service counter. The balls are poured into the top of what resembles a pinball machine standing on end. A lever is flicked and the balls zigzag at random down the face, past rows and rows of pins. Little wheels, cups and gates score points as the balls go past. If enough points are scored, they can be cashed in for prizes such as electric razors, toasters, sweets, fans and cigarettes.

It is considered to be relaxing for the mind and body after a hard day's work, but I've always found it to be the opposite. The long rows of machines with patrons shoulder-to-shoulder, the noise of the rattling steel balls, bells ringing and buzzers going off are disorientingly chaotic.

Once we entered the large, centrally heated room, my umbrella friend turned to me with a short bow and said, 'My name is Masa, please come out of the cold and have a drink.'

'Yeah okay, Masa. My name is Brian, I could do with one, thanks.'

Leading the way down between the crowded rows of machines with people intently watching the path of the balls, he entered a plush office at the rear. In the sudden quietness after he had closed the double-glazed, soundproof door, my new friend Masa stepped behind a well-stocked bar, enquiring over his shoulder, 'Scotch, rum, brandy, Brian?'

'Rum — neat please, Masa,' I answered through chattering teeth. My feet felt like two blocks of ice. Masa had a good grasp of the English language and he asked me, 'Do you like horse racing, Brian?'

'Yes, mate, I have been known to put a bit on the geegees.' I had to explain what geegees were and he thought it was very funny.

'What do you think of my gee-gee?' Masa asked, pointing to the very large painting of a racehorse that dominated the office.

'Wow, you own a racehorse?' I asked, walking over for a closer look and reading a brass engraving that read, Hoshi-no Hikari.

'Starlight,' he said simply.

We talked about golf, another of his expensive sports, until the parlour closed at midnight. He told me how he owned the whole complex and, after switching off the lights, drove me home in his new imported Jaguar.

Feeling no pain now after the rums, I shouted, 'Banzai!' as he drove away.

'Sayonara,' he laughingly replied.

*

The following night, I called in at the little bar in a tiny side street to see my Japanese mates, Kusaki, Hiro and Shigiji; the latter known as Ninja because of his appearance. I had found this bar one summer's day and was astonished when I looked inside to see that the barmen were all wearing genuine Australian rugby league football jumpers. Being a Manly supporter, on my next trip I took a Manly Sea Eagles flag which, incredibly, they hung out the front, renaming the bar the 'Sea Eagles' (Shii Iigaru in Japanese). Anyway, there they were in their usual spot and they gave me a questioning kind of look as I came down the length of the bar.

'How's it going, boys?' I enquired. They usually found my way of saying things amusing, but none of them was smiling today. Hiro hesitantly asked, 'Was that you drinking with THAT pachinko owner last night?' then self-consciously looked down into his beer.

'Yes,' I answered in surprise. News certainly travels fast around here, I thought.

'He is bad man. Be careful of him,' Hiro continued.

'Oh nonsense. Hiro, old mate, he could not have been nicer. Why, he even drove me back to the hotel.'

'Be careful,' Ninja whispered in a cautious way, looking around the bar.

*

Two weeks later, I was back in Fukuoka and dropped in to see Masa at the pachinko parlour. I gave him the stuffed koala he had asked me to bring.

'Hi there, Masa.'

'Konnichi-wa, Brian-san,' Masa replied with a sideways look I didn't understand. Pouring me a drink he casually asked, 'What are you doing tonight?'

'Nothing planned. What do you suggest?'

He stared at me for several seconds before answering. 'Come out with me and my girlfriend, Mazumi, and we will show you a side of life you don't know about.'

Why not? This could be interesting, I thought, swirling my Scotch around in the glass. It was a narrow street — so narrow I could touch both sides with my hands outstretched, and it was dimly lit. Masa stopped at the entrance, looking up and down the street before he entered. This should have given me vibes about it all, as I recalled the fellow at the end of the street as we entered. I was later to realise he was a 'cockatoo' (lookout). The building turned out to be an undertaker's parlour with a number of elaborately carved caskets stacked in a corner, shrines, funeral paper-money, candles, scrolls, incense and all the paraphernalia of the trade filling the small store.

Masa was greeted by fifteen of his friends, all with fierce looks on their faces. They were treating Masa with a great deal of caution and deference as if he was some kind of leader. As they grouped around him, deep in discussion, the tension built as every now and then Masa slammed his fist down on the nearest coffin for emphasis. It was then that I noticed for the first time, the tattoo on the inside of his wrist. All the other men had one too. Hiro's warning came to mind. Be careful.

Good heavens! It hit me like a blow to the ribs that this was some kind of organisation, maybe even terrorists. Sitting on a couch in the corner, Mazumi came over and sat next to me, inching along until she was very close and putting her hand on my leg. I looked down and there on her wrist was the same tattoo. The whole thing was getting out of control. Mazumi's hand was moving up my leg and I leapt a foot in the air. I thought, If Masa sees what's going on, I am in deep shit. I've got no idea where he thinks I fit into this organisation, but I'm not going to hang around to find out.

'Excuse me, Mazumi, I'll be right back,' I said, squeezing past her and heading for the toilet. I found it down a dark hallway and, closing the door, was relieved to see it was a Western toilet. There was a push-up window and I was further relieved that there were no bars on the outside. Standing on the toilet seat and unlocking the window, I slid it up without a sound. I leapt onto the cistern, clambered out, and fell head-first into years of accumulated rubbish in the dark alley. I picked myself up and made my way down the alley to the left with my hands held out in front. It was a dead end! I stumbled back the other way, but it was blocked. I realised it wasn't an alley at all but a light shaft. What next?

I'd no sooner muttered this when the toilet window

was slammed down and locked. Then it started to snow again. My eyes were adjusting to the dark now, with reasoning returning. Opposite was a window set low down and, getting my fingers under the frame, I was able to raise it slightly before it jammed. Panic returned and brute force soon had it up. I climbed in, falling into a bathtub full of hot water for it was indeed a bathroom. I opened the door, and there seated on the wooden floor around a low kotatsu table was a surprised family eating dinner, their chopsticks frozen and forgotten half-way to their open mouths.

I bowed from the waist as I made my way, dripping bath water on the polished floor. I brightly said, 'Good evening.' They all just sat there with puzzled expressions on their faces, looking from the bathroom then back to me. No worries. I was through and into the street heading away at a fast jog, soaking wet and hoping the 'mob' was not lurking in the street waiting for me. Those poor people are probably still wondering where the hell I came from.

There was no way I was going to tell my mates in the bar about it and have to put up with the 'I told you so' looks.

Several trips went by and Keisuki and I were eating champon, a popular Nagasaki noodle dish, in a restaurant, when he casually said, 'Hey Brian, you know Masa, who gave you a lift home that night?'

'Yes, what about him?'

'He had his pachinko parlour burnt down by a rival gang. We told you he was a bad man.'

99. My Mate, Mick

A few Singapore Gin Slings at the sleezy Garden of Eden Bar & Grill, and Mick, a mate of mine, had talked me into going with him to the New World Fun Park.

Prior to flying, Mick had been a jackaroo on a station in the outback. He was only five-feet-seven-inches (170cm) tall, but with a stocky build and as hard as nails. Easy-going, live-for-the-moment Mick had seen a few battles in his time. The scars on his face and the flattened, off-centre nose testified to his wins and losses.

We arrived at New World and Mick made a beeline for the taxi dancer hall. It was an open-air affair with a very large raised dance floor made of highly polished teak, surrounded by palm trees, and softly lit by swaying Chinese lanterns strung above the area to give the place a romantic air. The mandatory revolving mirrored ball glittered as it splashed fragmented light in all directions above the dancers.

One end of the establishment was taken up by a well-stocked bar with rattan stools and huge fans humming flat-out, giving the impression the dancers were dancing in a gale. The long sides had tiered seats for spectators to sit, with the fourth side occupied by the taxi dancers, sitting in little cubicles with a half door and a number on the front. The girls were all decked out in beautiful cheongsams with splits up the left side and flowers and charms plaited into their shiny, jet-black hair.

Now, for those who have never been to the New World, before entering the dance hall a book of six tickets was purchased for three Singapore dollars to dance, and dance ONLY with the girls in the boxes.

'No time to waste,' Mick said. He had put on his best Hawaiian beach shirt especially for the occasion and headed for box number eleven. Inside, it turned out, was the girl he always came to dance with. These girls were professional dancers, so no matter how poor your dancing skills were, they made you look and feel like Fred Astaire, assisted by a terrific twelve-piece orchestra dressed in blue tuxedos, playing the latest hits.

My mate Mick was dancing around with Number Eleven, and I was with her girlfriend, when a big, rough, tattooed sailor grabbed Mick's collar, pulling him up short and declaring, 'Righto, Aussie, that's my girl, so piss off.'

The look that Mick gave him should have warned him of trouble. It warned me and I was ten paces away. Maybe he had been drinking or was not very observant. Number Eleven and Mick glided off, doing some fancy steps around the floor, the big belligerent sailor never taking his eyes off little Mick from the side-line. Suddenly, he lunged at Mick as he glided past, grabbing his sleeve, and pulled hard. It tore right off in his hand. Mick's favourite shirt ripped. Now there was going to be trouble.

'What do you think of that, shorty?' the sailor said, still holding the jagged shirt sleeve in one hand, and throwing a tremendous right with the other, which, had it landed, would have put Mick over by the satay stalls.

Barely moving, Mick dodged the blow, following it up by kicking the sailor with the point of his shoe right in the crotch. The scream that followed silenced the band and all eyes were on my mate. The sailor had dropped to his knees, cupping his groin in both hands. This put his face in direct line with the straight left that sent his upper dentures clattering across the floor, ending up in the corner amongst the pot plants. An upper cut and three short belts to the ribs followed, which must have been heard out on Orchard Road. He keeled over. Mick, stepping nimbly sideways, moved off with Number Eleven around the floor as though it was an everyday occurrence. I also kept an eye on the troublemaker who had been dragged out of the way to the edge of the floor.

The sailor staggered to his feet with any thought of fighting knocked out of him, and wove his way out of the place.

'That will teach him to muscle in on my girl,' cried Mick from across the floor. I saw him in a new light; a handy mate indeed to have around.

*

Several years passed and Mick and I met up occasionally with each other in different parts of the world. Then he suddenly disappeared. It was rumoured that he had huge gambling debts in Sydney, threats were made, and Mick had done the moonlight flit.

He had been on a normal trip to San Francisco with a two-day stopover in Honolulu. When call-time came to operate the flight, there was no sign of him. Investigation of his room revealed none of his personal effects, but all his uniforms, manuals — everything belonging to the airline — were laid out. Nothing was heard of him from then on.

A couple of years later, crossing the road in Honolulu outside the Bank of Hawaii, who should be walking towards me from the other side of the road but Mick. He saw me and made signs not to stop –as we passed on Kalahaua Avenue, he said out of the corner of his mouth, 'G'day Brian.'

'How yer goin', Mick?' I responded ... and he was gone.

100. World of Music

Lee Wok's World of Music store always did a brisk business with airline crews staying at the old Lion City Hotel just around the corner.

The Lion City Hotel had been commandeered as

headquarters for the Japanese army in Singapore during World War II. Directly opposite, across the peaceful playing fields, is the YMCA, and it had been used by the Japanese as their interrogation centre. The locals called it the Building of Terror. We also had a name for the ageing Lion City, unaffectionately calling it 'Cockroach Castle' because of the large, red-winged roaches that roamed uninvited around the place. It was the only hotel we stayed in that I saw tin saucers of water placed under the bed legs to stop the big cockies from crawling into bed with guests. Placed under the bed by the room maids was an enamel jug of water to refill the little moats as the humid heat evaporated the water. It was always wise to check before retiring that the bed was away from the wall and the saucers were filled.

Anyway, working at the World of Music as a shop assistant was Kim. She was tall for a girl, nearly six feet. A mixture of Chinese and Indian, with long, shiny, jet-black hair framing a rather plain face, but boy oh boy, what a body. Kim wore clinging, brightly coloured cheongsams, and the crews flocked there to ogle at her, always ending up being talked into buying a record or two.

Lee Wok was one of the dying breeds of Chinese who stuck to the old style of dress, attired as he usually was in full-length black robes and gold slippers. He was also very tall, stick-thin, had a mouth full of gold teeth, and sported a long, wispy, white beard. He would saunter out into the shop with his hands shoved up the opposite wide sleeves and a ghastly gold grin as if he was having a secret joke with us.

It became a contest among the crews to see who would be first to win Kim's favours, but although Kim was friendly with everyone, she never went out with anyone. Alan Bushell, of the Water Tower in Karachi fame, appeared on the scene and took it on himself to be in charge of mission impossible. Look out, Kim!

Over a period of time, it was discovered that BOAC (British Overseas Airways Corporation) also had a contender and things were hotting up between the airlines with bets on who was going to win the day. The battle was on.

The day arrived when Alan finally broke down the barriers and Kim weakened, accepting an invitation to dinner at the then-fashionable Pavilion restaurant in Carn Hill.

This was a lovely, old-world restaurant on the first floor of a building (now the railway station). It was decorated like a cricket pavilion. The walls were painted with scenes of English country greens — Edwardian cricketers sporting waxed moustaches with bats under their arms chatting with ladies in long dresses, straw hats and parasols. There were lots of lattice panels and many balustrades which separated the tables for privacy. Even the waiters wore cricket apparel and chequered caps. Ah, yes, it oozed character. So, Kim and Alan had dinner there.

Alan was constantly pestered from then on by

the crew wanting to know how he got on with Kim and when was he going to see her again. Alan would grumpily tell them to mind their own business and 'all bets' were off. Everybody thought that poor Alan had met his match and Kim had given him the flick.

One evening, after a particularly hard day's flying, the crew went across to the Straits Bar for a few drinks before retiring. The usual banter was going on, with Alan copping a lot of flak. The double-lemon, Hart rum and Cokes were taking their toll and must have loosened Alan's tongue, because in a moment of weakness, he blurted out, 'Why me? Kim's not her real name — his name is Ken.'

Trade in the music shop dwindled after this piece of news travelled like wildfire, with none of the fellas wanting to be seen talking to a transvestite in case intentions were misinterpreted.

The secret spread and a few months later, World of Music closed down. Lee Wok took his secret weapon to another location. The shop re-opened under new management as Stitches Tailor Shop and also did a roaring trade with air crew.

101. Not Bloody Going

A bearer at Speedbird House in Karachi was sitting on the verandah cleaning shoes as I walked by.

'How yer going, mate?' I asked.

He looked up with rheumy red eyes and replied, 'I'm not bloody going, but I wish I was bloody going out of this stinking rotten place,' and went on cleaning shoes.

102. Happy Birthday, Mrs O'Connor

I was preparing the aircraft for the flight from Sydney to San Francisco when the traffic officer came onboard to tell me he was going to bring on Mrs O'Connor. She had been upgraded to first-class by management because it was her birthday — not any old birthday — her hundredth. A special birthday cake was put on and the crew, before starting dinner, sang 'Happy Birthday' to her. She loved it. I was about to start serving breakfast the next morning when the captain came on the public address system to tell the passengers that he had a special guest on board, and started to sing 'Happy Birthday' to her.

We have already done that, I said to myself — then I stopped dead. He's right. We had crossed the International Dateline and gone back a day. How about that? Not only one hundred, but one hundred twice.

In a quiet moment during the flight, I asked Mrs O'Connor what her secret recipe was for her long life, expecting the same old answer: Don't smoke, don't drink and lots of exercise. She smiled at me with her twinkling blue eyes and said, 'Keep breathing!'

103. Speech Therapy

After winning the election in 1972, the Labor Government, headed by Mr Gough Whitlam, chartered a 707 aircraft for a visit to the powers of Europe. Cabin crew management called me into the office to inform me I would be the chief steward on this historic flight. (Remember the other historic flights?)

'Historic?' I croaked. 'What now?'

'There's only one small thing you have to do before going,' the manager continued.

Oh yeah, I thought.

'It's okay, it's just a little speech therapy.'

'What?' I exclaimed.

The speech therapy consisted of simply greeting the Whitlams at the aircraft door with: 'Good morning, Mr Prime Minister and Mrs Whitlam. Welcome aboard.' (My accent is pure Australian.)

'Ten little words. No problem,' I said.

Ten little words took over an hour to master to their liking. I was thinking, What about the rest of the journey? Back to the Australian drawl it seems. Yet another dopey company idea.

From then on it was a delightful time with them; in fact, it was the best three-weeks trip I ever did — more like a holiday than work. The sectors around Europe were very short, about an hour, requiring only simple silver service, like morning tea, afternoon high tea, soup, or just cocktails, then get off.

Gough took a liking to me and invited me to one or two of the official lavish dinners with Margaret. A memorable one was hosted by the prime minister of Greece at the palace. For this extravagant affair I wore my new white sharkskin suit from Singapore, and white shoes — the works.

While seated with the Whitlams at this state dinner, the local newspaper journalists waited impatiently outside. Dinner was followed by traditional Greek dancing (Zorba), then — obviously for us — some light dance music.

I asked Margaret if she would care to dance with me and it was at that moment, as we danced around, that the press were allowed in for a short time. Yes — they took pictures of Margaret and me. At least one of the newspapers got it all horribly wrong because, when I opened the hotel door next morning, there on the carpet was the local morning paper with me on the front page.

Above the picture in large letters was, 'Welcome to Gough and Margaret Whitlam, Prime Minister of Australia'. This was quickly corrected in the next edition.

Gough thought it was the funniest thing he had ever

seen and laughed about it for days. They were great company.

104. Bunny's Foot

'Hi, Bunny,' I said, dropping down on the warm Waikīkī sand beside him.

Looking up from reading his book, he drawled, 'G'day, Brian.' I glanced down and noticed the mess his left foot and leg were in from a past injury. Even though it had healed well, it was pretty mangled.

'Gee, that must have hurt. What happened?'

Bunny, who was my captain, gazed out to sea and said, 'It's a long story, Brian, and happened a long time ago.'

The Lancaster bomber KC492 was caught in the blinding glare of the 10,000-candle-power German searchlights over Brest in France. They had dropped their load of bombs and were on their way home when the interior of the aircraft was lit up brighter than daylight, momentarily blinding Bunny and his crew.

Bunny threw the bomber all over the sky, trying to avoid the deadly beam as flak seemed to lazily fly up to meet them. The sky was now alight with blinding searchlights, burning aircraft and blazing buildings down below. Creaking and groaning to stresses far beyond the manufacturer's specifications, the Lancaster at last avoided the deadly light just as a blast of flak sent shrapnel up through the floor of the cockpit and out through the windscreen.

A searing pain ran up Bunny's left leg and, when he leaned down and ran his hand down inside his sheepskin-lined flying boot, he was amazed at the amount of blood on his hand when he looked at it in the glow of the instrument panel.

The return journey to England with Bunny at the controls was accomplished in lapses of semi-consciousness and near-unconsciousness. Each time Bunny looked like passing out, the navigator shook him awake. It seemed to be endless. Then out in the distance the white cliffs of the English coast appeared.

It was decided, because Bunny was lapsing in and out of consciousness more often, that they would land at the nearest airfield, which happened to be an American base at Beaulieu.

Continually having to be shaken, Bunny put the aircraft down in one of the worst possible landings. Watched by both air and ground crews, the smouldering wreck rolled off the runway and onto the grass verge. The stillness was eerie. A jeep screeched to a stop and out jumped an American captain.

As Bunny was being carried past, sprawled out on a stretcher, covered in blood, the American shouted out in a loud voice, 'That's the worst doggone landing I've ever seen. Who was responsible for it?'

The engineer, who was also passing by, heard the remark and, with the flick of his thumb, indicated Bunny, saying, 'He did,' with admiration. They reckon the look on the American's face was priceless.

Bunny did forty-three bombing runs to Germany and flew with 617 — the Dambusters squadron.

105. The Weekender

For the third time, I looked at the address I'd written down on a scrap of paper. Yep, it's definitely number sixty-nine. I've got to be in the wrong street as sixty-nine is definitely not a bookshop. It's a brothel and doing a brisk trade going by the number of fellas trooping in and out. In fact, when I looked closely, most of the places in the street seemed to be on the game. Girls in tight-fitting T-shirts and short dresses were sitting on most of the front stone doorsteps with legs splayed and murmuring things they would like to do to you.

Bugger this, I'm off.

It was then that I noticed the man hunched over a hissing kerosene stove under a staircase at number seventy-three. 'Hey, mate, is this Albion Street?'

Mr Lee informed me in broken English, 'This Knock Street.' *Aptly named*, I thought. 'Albion Street over there,' he added, pointing with the tongs he was using to turn the small fish frying in a fire-blackened pan. With his wife and two little girls, he lived in these sordid, cramped conditions under the stairway that had been roughly partitioned off by the owner of the tenanted building. The owner even had the gall to ask for rent to exist in this coop with no toilet, washing facilities or even a stove.

Mr Lee told me that they had only stayed on because it was cheap and, importantly, close to the harbour where he went fishing each day to supply food for the family. Through all this, the Lees had not lost faith in their religion, and there on the wall was a crucifix with a single, yellow daisy tucked behind it.

Not much hope for the little girls here, I thought to myself. They are sure to end up on the 'game'.

As I walked to the bookshop, I considered how we take our good life in Australia for granted. Those who have travelled anywhere overseas all come back with a different feeling and a more patriotic view of our easy-going way of life.

On the corner of Albion Street was a small stone Catholic church, built in miniature Gothic-style. The thought occurred to me that maybe their care group could help the Lees. I also had a feeling that Mr Lee was too proud to ask for help himself. The wrought-iron gate squealed in protest as I pushed it open and again as it was shut. A middle-aged man with a lined face and eyes that said, I've seen it all, answered my knock on the studded door. He introduced himself as Alfonce Forenze and we talked about the Lees' problem. Alfonce, with a smile, said to leave it with him and he would make a few enquiries.

Several weeks later, back in Manila, I called in at the centre to see if anything had eventuated for the Lees.

'Remember me?' I asked when Alfonce opened the door. 'How did you get on with the Lee family?'

Alfonce ushered me into his cluttered office, chuckling to himself. 'Ah, yes. The Lee von Trapp family,' he said, indicating for me to sit down.

'Why do you say that, Alfonce? They looked to me to be in dire need of help.'

'Indeed, indeed they are, Brian,' Alfonce said, still chuckling to himself. 'And we did all we could for them. Have you heard the phrase, "biting the hand that feeds you"?'

'What happened?' I asked, sighing deeply.

Alfonce returned to his desk, shuffling papers about and, in between bouts of laughter, said, 'We found a Good Samaritan out by the stadium who gave them free accommodation. He even helped them move in. Several days later, Mr Lee called back here at the office and enquired if we could continue paying the rent on the old staircase accommodation so they could get away for the weekends and do some fishing.'

106. Lost and found — mainly lost

You would not believe the number of people over the years who apprehensively approached me in flight to tell me they had lost their passport, money wallet, handbag, coat — the list was endless. I remember finding a wallet on the bench in the rear toilet one night with about US$5,000 stuffed in it. I locked it in a drawer up at the front and waited for the panicked passenger to appear, knowing it would not be long.

The big, crew-cut Canadian burst through the curtain demanding to know if someone had found his wallet.

'Indeed. I found it in the toilet,' I said, and asked him to tell me what was in it. After establishing it was definitely his, I handed it over. He snatched it from my hand, counted the money, shoved it in his hip pocket and walked away. Forget about a little something for finding it; he didn't even say 'thank you'. I was brought up to believe that honesty is the best policy. After this treatment, it took me some time to believe it.

*

The brown paper bag was lying in the aisle during the first-class lunch service. With both hands carrying a tray laden with cups, plates and cutlery, I gave it a good hard kick back towards the galley area.

I picked it up and was about to throw it in the rubbish bin when it split open, revealing six bundles of American one-hundred-dollar bills. The seat near where it had been lying was occupied by two small boys, aged between ten and twelve years old, playing a video game.

I approached the father of the two boys who had boarded the flight in Bahrain in the Arabian Gulf dressed in the full Arab garb.

'Have you lost any money?' I asked.

He looked down at my hands holding the now taped-up bag and exploded.

'Will you boys take more care of your pocket money!' He took it from me and tossed it over the seat where it again landed on the floor. It was still on the floor when I got off in Rome. It took me longer this time to believe the honesty policy.

*

A passenger once asked me if I would, for fifty dollars, put my hand into the toilet to retrieve his gold watch, which had fallen in.

'Not for fifty thousand dollars, mate!'

Would you ever actually wear it again? I wouldn't.

107. I Know the King

Captain Chaos was with me in Bangkok when we went to a night club called Siam Nights in sleazy Potpong Road. At around about 10pm the floor show started and — wouldn't you know it — it was a strip show. Now, I should explain that this happened many years ago when this kind of entertainment was illegal in Siam (Thailand) and those caught were prosecuted.

Anyway, halfway through the educational performance, the police raided the club, bursting in through the front door. The management flipped the electricity switch, plunging the place into complete darkness and causing a stampede for the rear exits.

Everybody was pushing and shoving, and to my amazement, Chaos started yelling out not to worry, he knew the king. What difference that was going to make? I never found out. We were lucky not only in getting out alive, but escaping arrest. Strangely, I was later to meet the king and his son who, ultimately, was to become the next king on his father's death years later. When they boarded our flight, I was very tempted to ask the king if he knew Chaos, but then thought better of it. Wiser to let sleeping dogs lie.

108. Cloud Nine

'I tell you, it's true,' I said to the crew sitting around drinking in the crew-room. 'Don and I have just come from there.'

We were walking around in the Mong Kok area of Hong Kong when we saw the sign on a door saying 'Cloud Nine'. Thinking it was a bar, we entered and approached a makeshift bar in the corner. A scantily clad young girl appeared with the familiar click-clack of wooden sandals on a tiled floor.

'What you want?' she demanded.

'We would like a couple of rum and Cokes, please,' I said.

'No rum.'

'Well, vodka tonics.'

'No vodka.'

'What kind of bar is this? Have you any beer?'

'Only got Tiger beer.'

'Okay. Two of them.'

The girl bent over to take two beers from a bucket full of ice, showing more of herself, if that was possible.

It was obvious we were not welcome as she flipped off the bottle tops, which landed on the floor, rolling round and round. Again, exposing more of herself, she reached up to take two filthy glasses off a shelf, which we ignored.

'Something funny going on here,' Don said, adding, 'Maybe it's a knock house. I've been watching the locals coming in and going down to the back wall and putting coins in a slot, then standing close up against the wall.'

'I think it's a peep show,' I suggested.

Getting up from the table, we casually walked down for a closer look and almost dropped our beers when we saw that the holes in the wall were at crotch height.

They were putting their penises in these putrid holes and having them played with behind the wall. I would have given a day's pay to have a look at the other side of that wall.

Now, before you race off to buy a ticket to Hong Kong — 'Cloud Nine' has gone, closed down by the Health Department. I wonder why?

109. G'day, Mate

Communication between Management and cabin crew in the 1960s and 1970s was mainly by typed memos put into our files. After sign-on, we were required to read them before we flew off into the wide blue yonder. Face-to-face was usually reserved for when we were in trouble and were 'on the mat'.

Some memos were interesting, some informative, some plain stupid, such as:

Do not sing or whistle the popular song of the 1960s Hava Nagila in Cairo, Egypt, with tensions between them and Israel escalating.

When travelling in a taxi or tuk tuk in Bangkok, drivers take a dim view of passengers who tap them on the shoulder — that's where their guardian angel resides.

It is advisable and wise if involved in a traffic accident in Iran in a taxi — to run. Otherwise, there is a good possibility you will have to finance anyone injured, as technically you caused the accident when you hired the taxi.

When in Bahrain and conversing with someone, do not point your feet directly at the person. It is considered poor manners.

It has come to the notice of management that an increasing number of crew have lowered the set standard of address to passengers boarding and on board the aircraft. Uncouth sayings such as 'G'day mate', 'good on yer', 'how yer goin'?', 'fair dinkum', 'she'll be right', 'bonzer', 'yer not wrong', 'ripper, sport', and many more are to cease immediately or disciplinary action will be taken.

What on earth are they thinking about? Not only is it true blue Australian, it's an Australian airline, crewed by — yeah, Aussies. Passengers boarding the aircraft after being away from the lucky country for any length of time all told us how great it was to hear the down-under accent again.

The very next trip, I decided to make a point. The

flight was called at Singapore and the first person to board was a middle-aged man, loaded down with shopping bags.

'G'day mate, been shopping?' I drawled.

'Too right,' he replied, 'flat out like a lizard drinking.'

110. The Upgrade

I had just closed the left front door of the Boeing, with a fourteen-hour flight from Los Angeles to Sydney ahead of us. Both Business and Economy were chockers, but first-class was surprisingly half empty. At that moment I became aware of a racket going on in the middle of the economy-class cabin. I made my way down, wondering why a woman was standing in the aisle, not seated for take-off.

'I'm not sitting next to that for fourteen hours,' the haughty English woman with hands on hips hissed at me, pointing to the passenger who was seated next to her. 'That' to whom she was referring was a well-dressed, very embarrassed, middle-aged, African-American gentleman, looking down at the carpet with the whole of economy-class passengers tuned in.

I sized up the situation in a flash. She's looking for an upgrade at the expense of this poor fellow. The African-American man looked up at me with sad eyes as I said,

'Could you step out into the aisle, please?'

He did so with a look of dread in his eyes. 'Follow me,' I said to the man, leaving the English woman open-mouthed.

'There you are, madam, problem solved,' I said to a round of applause from the surrounding, now hostile passengers, all glaring at the woman.

Twenty minutes later, the man, now seated in first-class, was sampling for the first time in his life caviar on blinis with chilled Russian vodka. This was followed by full first-class silver service, and a bed to retire in, all the way to Sydney.

He told me later in the flight that he thought he was going to be off-loaded. I know which passenger I would have enjoyed immensely doing that to.

I filled in an incident report and thought no more about it — until I ran into the person who handled the report back in Sydney. He was also appalled at this man's treatment by another passenger and decided to take it to Management, who promptly upgraded his return flight ticket.

Sometimes the airline got it right — but there is a sneaky suspicion it was simply good public relations on Management's part, as that man would talk about our airline for years and years to come.

111. Mal's Wig

Anybody who flew Qantas — even for a short time — knew about Mal and his antics. He was as bald as a billiard ball and wore a wig; well, sometimes. He was also a master of disguise. I only flew with him a couple of times, and that was plenty.

The first time I flew with him, he was impeccably dressed and bald. Before the dinner service, he dimmed the lights down low for 'his act' and served the hot savouries in the wig. First course: wig, droopy moustache and glasses; second course: grey beard, false nose, pince-nez glasses and stooped over.

On it went and then, when working in the galley, I heard a loud, nasal Australian exclaim, 'How many bloody stewards are on this plane?' Mal was waiting for this and would then reveal himself, to the amazement and delight of the passengers. Yeah, he was a performer, and he once told me how he was in Vaudeville before flying. Ah ha, does this tell us something? Sometimes he would raise his arm for some reason — maybe putting a bag in the overhead locker with the wig shoved up his short-sleeved shirt.

112. Glamour in the Air

On the old 'egg beater' aircraft years ago (DC3, DC4, Fockers, Electras and Constellations) the air quality was not nearly as good as on modern planes. Can you believe it? They had curtains on the windows with little tassels. Modern air-conditioners, purifiers and non-smoking laws have made flying more comfortable now and much cleaner.

Whenever I returned from a trip flying in the good old days on the 'egg beaters', my children would run to give me a hug, then one of them would exclaim, 'Dad, you smell like an aeroplane.' A cocktail of smells from aviation fuel, cigarettes, passengers, food, toilets, sweat, air sickness, bad breath and smelly feet were the culprits.

Sounds glamorous, doesn't it? To think that we had to fight tooth-and-nail against hundreds of applicants to be chosen to become cabin crew. I wonder how many would have backed out after reading this little enlightener? Even so, by golly, we had a lot of fun.

There was one other smell that I have not mentioned, caused by the fear of flying. I have smelled it on a few occasions with people sitting there terrified. It is a distinctive, but not unpleasant, smell that horses and wild beasts ... and chief stewards can detect.

113. Soap

When I began flying, long trips such as London could take up to twenty-three days. This included up to ten different first-class hotels we would stay at in different countries.

Of course, one of the complimentary luxuries the hotels supplied was soap. These mini-size soaps were top quality, which the makers hoped you would like, and in future, buy. It was human nature that one would throw the unused complimentary mini-soaps into one's suitcase. Multiply three cakes by ten hotels — you have half a suitcase of soap — be honest now — EVERYBODY took it, but none would admit to it. After a particularly good, long trip where we all got along well, the captain invited the whole crew to his harbourside home for a barbecue, and nearly all the crew turned up. We were all sitting around having a cocktail and a good time, when my seven-year-old son, Bart, went to the toilet. He raced back into the room and excitably exclaimed for all to hear, 'Hey, Dad! They have big soap.'

114. Irene

Before airlines tightened up the rules on security, which forbid entry to the Boeing 707 flight deck by anyone except crew, it was quite common for the captain to invite passengers up to the cockpit for a look-see.

This particular day, the captain casually enquired if there were any VIPs, people of interest or any 'good sorts' (pretty girls) on board.

'I'll be back,' I said.

In Business there was a lovely couple with their daughter, Irene, about ten years old. She had Down's Syndrome — a lovely, sweet little girl with the debilitating effects of her condition. I took her up to see the captain. Full marks to the technical crew. They treated Irene to the full tour. Ken, the engineer, showed her all the dials and different blinking lights. The captain called her forward to look out the front windscreen and down out of the portside window, and explained the controls. The navigator, not to be left out, showed her the periscope to look at the stars.

I admired the way they handled this situation and when I indicated it was time to go back to her seat, the captain said, 'Let her stay a little while.'

The parents were getting a little apprehensive about the time she was away until I told them the situation. They burst out crying that we should show such interest in their little girl, Irene. I flew with that captain several times later, and each time I gave him the little extras from the first-class galley, which he deserved.

115. Shanty Hygiene

During my training, the hygiene course warned us about not eating salads, cold rice, smorgasbord meals and the like in places such as Pakistan, Iran and India, not to mention Ceylon (Sri Lanka); however, the trainer didn't mention ... well, let me tell you.

One hot summer afternoon, after going for a walk in the chaotic streets of New Delhi in India, with the soft breeze blowing crap of all descriptions in my face, I was looking forward to a stiff drink and a shower.

On returning to the five-star hotel, I went up to my room to find the door wide open and the cleaning lady inside giving the bathroom the once-over. I stood transfixed to see her cleaning around the bend of the toilet with my toothbrush. She immediately put it behind her back but, looking in the mirror, there it was with days of filth hanging off it. She obviously intended to wash it and put it back on the bench.

I telephoned the manager who promptly came up. When told what she had done, incredibly, he started to defend the girl, saying the cleaners were employed from the shanty villages on the outskirts of the city. He went on to say that their hygiene was not up to the standard of Westerners. No apology was offered.

I began to leave out a disposable toothbrush for the cleaners to do with as they wished, while mine was safely locked in my suitcase. Maybe they thought 'hygiene' was a tall girl (high Jean).

Some of the hotel room maids in the South Pacific islands think it is a great joke to catch a large, red-winged cockroach and trap it between the bed pillows. You get into bed and ... AHHHHHH!

116. A Child's View

I wonder how many other air crew with families ever considered what their young children thought of them when they were only three or four years old. With our constant coming and going, it must have been very confusing for them.

One time, it had been a very long, harrowing trip with full loads, and a chief steward who rode us all the way for no good reason except to boost his ego. I was glad it was over. We were first to land in Sydney after the 6 am curfew and I was home and in bed before the kids had even woken up.

It was early afternoon when I woke up to hear my two

little girls, aged three and five, open the bedroom door and creep over to the side of the bed. I kept my eyes closed and waited to find out what they would do. My five-year-old, Suzanne, leaned forward, carefully lifted up one eye lid and exclaimed, 'Hey, Mummy, he's in there!'

117. Calcutta (Kolkata)

Flying into Calcutta one afternoon, the hostess, Kathy, sidled up to me and said, 'You know, Brian, India is the only country where I wash my hands before I go to the toilet!'

118. Chicken or Beef

Another harebrained idea that was approved of by management was the following: Why not bring down Thai nationals from Thailand on three-month visas and employ them as cabin crew on a fraction of the wage paid to Australian crew? No incentive here!

Great — it was approved. The trouble was, most of them were not fluent in English and there was no sign of any Australianisms such as 'G'day, mate,' or 'How yer going?'

They were extremely lackadaisical, and rightly so, as they were well aware that the Australians were better paid. Most of the answering of call bells was left to the regular, professional crew. A friend of mine told me how she was ashamed and embarrassed to work with them on the food trolleys. They only said three words all the way through the cabin — 'chicken or beef'.

Talk about lowering standards! Money seemed to be more important. Whoever thought this one up should be shown the door.

119. Free at Last

It was early one frosty winter's day in 1973 when we flew into Tehran, the capital of Iran, for four days. The crew transport picked us up at the airport and half an hour later we drove through the enormous wrought-iron gates, with high stone walls capped by broken glass bottles surrounding the old-world Park Hotel.

The hotel manager was waiting for us at reception to inform us that the government had declared they would abolish all forms of slavery at 10am that day. We were warned not to venture out into the streets as rioting and violence was expected to occur. I stayed up to watch the historic event through the window of my hotel room.

When 10am came, the roads and streets were full of

yelling, crying, singing, dancing, newly created citizens. As I watched at about midday, a low-flying aircraft flew across the city, dropping millions of pamphlets about the event. Several fluttered down right there on the patio — I still have one.

Later in the day, I woke up and threw open the curtains to drizzling rain. The same people had nowhere to go that night and were sleeping under awnings, in shop doorways, crowded onto the bandstand and under the She-oak trees in the park. On day two, it was a very sodden, hungry, subdued crowd wandering aimlessly around the city — and drizzling rain was predicted again that night. Day three: the holiday atmosphere was gone, replaced by a howling, angry mob with homemade placards, demanding as they marched through the streets that this bill of rights be rescinded.

I ventured out into the streets late in the afternoon and was appalled at the state of these simple people. A thousand times I was asked for money. There was one forlorn man sitting in the gutter, shivering with not even a shirt on. I gave him my light windcheater. The look on his face was priceless, and I hurried back to the warmth of the hotel. Many of these poor people had already gone back, pleading with their employers to be taken in again to their warm beds, with food and lodgings. Lots of these people had been born into this situation and knew no other way of life, with few or no possessions of their own. A new bill was very quickly drawn up, cancelling this proclamation, which was shoved under the nearest Persian carpet. Like many harebrained ideas proclaimed by parliaments and governments world-wide (without first thinking about the possible repercussions), this was a prime example of the consequences.

120. The Champion

In 1956, there was a Super-Constellation 1049 aircraft heading for London, which landed at Calcutta, India, for refuelling. On board in the hold was a prize-winning sheep dog on its way for breeding in Wiltshire in south-western England.

The engineer, after doing his check around the aircraft, looked in on the dog and decided to let it out for a run-about. It did a runabout alright — through a hole in the airport fence — and disappeared into the shanties bordering the airport.

The engineer was stunned. What to do? There were hundreds of dogs roaming around the tarmac, so he coaxed one of similar size and colour that looked half healthy into the cage, and the plane carried on to Old Blighty.

That flight crew kept it secret and waited anxiously for weeks for trouble to hit the fan — nothing came back. It can only be concluded it was that dog's lucky day, breeding away happily and cossetted like a silkworm.

Meanwhile, in Calcutta, the champion dog was also, with gay abandon, distributing champion genes willy-nilly.

121. Underpaid

The hotel where we stayed at in Bombay, India, on 'slips' (or what the Americans called 'layovers' — yeah, we won't go into that terminology) had a very nice hotel with pool and tennis court. I have a lot of beaut memories of playing on that court.

That day, Paul, with whom I usually played tennis, was running late so I decided to have a beer in the bar while I waited. It turned into two beers and a ham sandwich.

Paul eventually arrived and, while signing the bill, I casually asked the barman what barmen's wages were like. He looked at me with rheumy eyes and stunned me when he said my bill was more than a day's wages. I hadn't even glanced at the total while signing it. It ruined my tennis day.

122. Service with a Smile

Airlines throughout the world in the 1960s and 1970s were all striving to be up there at the top. All-important safety was top of the list of criteria for judging track records, then in-cabin service, engineering, dependability and price, in that order.

When I joined the airline in this era, at boarding time, there we would all be, decked out in white Eton jackets with polished brass buttons and epaulettes, black cummerbunds around our waists and snappy black bowties. We loved our job, so smiling came easily.

We seated passengers, hung their coats, stowed their cabin bags in the overhead shelf, gave them canned orange juice (we called it battery acid), newspapers, magazines, lollies in a basket to 'pop' the ears, and hot or cold towels, depending on the weather. All this was done before take-off; unlike some overseas airlines where it was a free-for-all when boarding, with no allocated seating plan and no pre-take-off service. I do understand that due to the upmarket, huge aircraft having up to eighty-odd rows, it would be impossible to give such service in the time allowed — but it was far, far better back then. No wonder Qantas was listed then as number one airline in the world.

123. Not Going

One day in the first-class cabin, I was chatting to the company director of a very well-known, large business firm. He began by bragging about his wealth — waterfront harbour mansion, yacht, vintage cars, etcetera.

I happened to remark, 'It's all very nice, but in the end, you can't take it with you.' He looked hard at me and exclaimed, 'If I can't take it with me, I'm not going.' He was not laughing.

124. The Side Show

Mr Ward, a tramway engineer, was seated in first-class and told me a story that really made me laugh. He was returning home after a problem-solving mission in East Asia. His company had received a complaint that their elevated (above road) monorail trams' wheel bearings on the right side were wearing out alarmingly fast compared to the ones on the left side. Mr Ward said his company could not figure out why, so they sent him out there to investigate.

After a full inspection of the wheel bearings, springs, brakes and suspension, he went for a ride on the elevated train and stood at the back to observe the ride.

He told me he immediately noticed how all the male passengers were crammed in on the right side, tilting the train over and putting extra pressure on the bearings. The tram, at one point, ran very close to a building at a tram stop.

A bordello and massage parlour of sorts was on the second storey of this building with very large, unobstructed picture windows.

Yes, the passengers had a front seat and clear view of the goings-on inside; even better if the tram had to stop at the station.

Mr Ward sorted it out at very little expense — lace curtains on the bordello's windows!

125. From Ties to T-shirts

Many years ago, in the 1950s and early 1960s era of the 'good old days', it was very expensive to fly anywhere — even locally.

It was expected that men would wear a suit, waistcoat, and collar and tie; women also dressed up in their finery (gloves, pearls and hats) to fly overseas to exciting places on the then state-of-the-art Super Constellation L-1049. This was long before mass tourism kicked in and ruined the experience with hordes of people everywhere.

Unfortunately, things have deteriorated greatly to the point where, nowadays, even some celebrities and important people are arriving at the aircraft door looking dishevelled, like they have just come from doing the gardening or working on their car.

126. The Yank

The crew jumpseat for Economy-Class (cattle class) on the Boeing 707 aircraft was at the aft door right next to the toilets. I have lost count of the number of times when sitting there, I would observe a lady come out of the small toilet heading back to her seat.

Because of the cramped and confined space in the toilet, some women didn't get it right, and would reappear with the back of their dress or skirt caught up in their stockings or pantyhose. I'd give the dress a yank as she went past and the woman's face would go from, 'How dare you!' to 'Thank you'. It was like being at The Follies.

127. The Captain's PA

I smile every time I think of the captain who regularly gave his PA 'Welcome Aboard' spiel: 'Weather is fine for our arrival, warm and sunny …' And finished off with, 'If there is anything you may desire during the flight, don't hesitate to call for a steward, and he will happily give it to you.'

128. Red

The airline had lots of colourful regulars flying and one chap comes to mind, nicknamed 'The Red Terror' because of his hair.

He had the ability to sum up people in a flash; he was very quick with smart-aleck answers and didn't suffer fools gladly. It was all done while smiling sweetly, covering himself against any complaints — and there would have been many.

I stood in the galley with Red one afternoon and watched as a tall cowboy, complete with white Stetson cowboy hat, coat with fringes front and back, string tie, belt buckle for winning a buck-jumping event, and South American tooled boots, climb out of his seat. He came down the aisle towards us with that curious sideways walk like John Wayne. He stopped at the galley and in a loud, booming drawl declared, 'Howdy boys, I'm from Texas.'

Quick as a flash, Red replied, 'Where the bloody hell is that?' The poor fellow slunk off, completely deflated.

129. Oh Ye of Little Faith

Sometimes, before boarding for a long flight, I would wander around under the Boeing 747 Jumbo, marvelling at the sheer size and bulk of it. Those Rolls Royce engines just don't look nearly large or powerful enough to thrust the plane into the air.

All up, weight (full complement of fuel, cargo, 400-odd passengers and crew, luggage, water and catering) was around 400,000 kgs. I would shake my head and think, It's just not possible and too ridiculous to even contemplate.

I would then climb on board, go about my pre-flight duties before departure, belt up for take-off and watch the unbelievable happen. Did Wilbur and Orville Wright have the same misgivings about their flimsy flying machine, Kitty Hawk?

130. Lexie

Lexie was great to work with. She was pretty, friendly, enthusiastic, with high levels of anticipation and very proud and grateful to have the job of flying as a hostie. She also had one small problem through no fault of her own.

Lexie, at five years old in 1943, together with her whole family, had been herded through the Gates of Hell, Auschwitz concentration camp. It left her with a horror of the wastage of food. I quite often flew with her and observed her during meal service, bringing back into the galley first-class dinner plates. Shaking her head, she scraped half-eaten steak, lobster and fish into the garbage bin — the wastage was enormous.

One day, Lexie looked at me with a sad look on her face and said, 'Look at that, this steak has hardly been touched.' She ate it then and there.

Poor Lexie. How are you, wherever you are?

131. Dawn Air-raid Siren

When we first began flying into Bahrain in the Arabian Gulf in the late 1960s and early 1970s, crews were billeted at the MET army barracks. This was long before the Gulf Hotel was built.

In the centre of the parade ground was an old, World War II air-raid siren with a crank handle to wind it up. That didn't last long.

The army removed the handle to stop tanked-up crew, who couldn't resist giving it a whirl, day and night .

132. The Best Job in the World

I hear all the time from crew who declare how lucky they were to be selected from thousands and thousands of applicants to be part of the cabin crew network.

In my case, I can confidently say I was over-the-top, super lucky. The notice that four stewards were required for overseas service appeared in the Sydney Morning Herald. The requirements were:

Height for weight:I am slim
Maximum height 5'10" (177.8 cm)I am 180.34 cm
Up to twenty-five years of ageI am twenty-six
Intermediate CertificateNo — I lied
Additional language is an advantageNo — again

I only had a part-time job at the time as a repossession agent. Still, George Watham, Phil Penn and Ted White at Qantas all saw the worth in me. I'll always be grateful — thank you, guys.

133. Cabaret

This true story has nothing to do with flying, but is just too good to be left out. We have all seen (well, I have anyway) or heard about, the sleazy cabarets in the South Seas and the Caribbean. Scantily-clad girls, smoke-filled dance venues, unhealthy-looking degenerates in dark glasses lounging about, and the awful smell of sin and debauchery.

Social dances all over Sydney in the 1960s sometimes

put on a cabaret dance — very much toned down, with a mirrored ball splashing lights all around, potted palms, a few decorations, the band all decked out in Hawaiian beach shirts and no sign of depravity.

One morning, we had a knock on the front door and standing there were four Bible people who, I might add, did a wonderful job.

We got talking and one of them asked me where my wife and I first met all those years ago.

'We met at a cabaret,' I replied.

They all looked at me in awe. 'You married a pole dancer?'

134. Nicknames

Not so much now, but in the 'good old days', the majority of crew had nicknames and you were very lucky if you got a kind one. Some were quite detrimental and insulting, and living with it would have been hard.

Did you know airlines also had nick names? Here is just a sample of some of the 'nice' ones:

SAS Airlines: Sex and Satisfaction

Pan Am: Pandemonium

British Airways: Bloody Awful

QANTAS: Queers and Nymphomaniacs Travelling as Stewards

Air India: The Curry Castle
American Airlines: Alcoholics anonymous
Trans World Airlines: Teeny Weeny Airlines.

135. Runway to Highway

I wonder how many passengers realise when they leave the international terminal in Singapore on the coach or in a taxi heading into town, that part of the highway they are travelling on was the old runway.

It also had another use. The Singaporeans were clever. Instead of jack-hammering the runway up, they decided they could use it if a crisis were to occur.

Simple: Take away the flower pots and boxes down the middle of the road, lower the tall street lights (hinged at the bottom) outwards and use the lights for runway lights. Bob's your auntie.

136. Heinui and the La Fayette

The Fiesta route to London via Papeete, Tahiti, Mexico City and Bermuda was only a twice-weekly service, so crews had four lovely days both north- and south-bound in Papeete, Polynesia, to enjoy ourselves.

Quite often, I hired a motorbike from 'Tahtite Motocyclettes' — yes, that's what the sign read. The business was housed in a ramshackle construction of four posts and wire netting. Palm fronds overlapped to form a roof. It looked like a chicken coop.

Big old fat Heinui, who owned this small business (incidentally Heinui is both a boy's and a girl's name), was usually found in amongst the jumble of haphazardly thrown cycles, sprawled out in a deckchair. He had the debilitating elephantiasis seen around Polynesia years ago. His testicles were the size of melons, which he wheeled about in a battered wheelbarrow. One day I forgot to bring my licence, so I gave him a laundry receipt, which he meticulously copied down.

Then, down in the risky, unsafe waterfront docks area, I found the La Fayette Night Club.

*

The builders must have gotten inspiration from the cycle shack as it was built on the same theme: rough and ready. About the size of a tennis court, it had posts dug into the ground to support the rusty corrugated-iron roof. Plaited palm fronds nailed on crossbeams, crawling with large cockroaches, formed the walls. The dance floor was dirt. Huge speakers blasted out raucous Tahitian music and a roughly sawn timber bar running along one wall did a roaring trade serving even rougher locally brewed rum about a week old. The tables and chairs were also made out of heavy, rough timber to withstand the 'incidents' — and there were many.

Patrons of this fine establishment were scantily dressed prostitutes, pimps, hit men, rough tattooed seamen, pick-pockets, those handy with a knife, on-the-run criminals, trouble-makers, thieves and gangsters — in fact, all the riff-raff of the south seas — and me. I loved going there.

The latrines were out the back, which were in a class all of their own. They were fashioned also of filthy, plaited palm fronds. House bricks were scattered on the dirt floor with heavy construction mesh thrown on top to walk on. No chain to pull here. An equally putrid, one-metre-high timber fence separated the girls from the boys. It was worse for the girls trying to balance on the mesh in high heel shoes — and the smell!

One trip in there instantly cured you of incontinence for the rest of the evening. Around 10pm, the French Foreign Legion would arrive all dressed up in smart uniforms and polished desert boots. The commanding officer, with a dispatch satchel tucked under his arm, would call for recruits from the now-drunken mob to join up and see the world — well, the deserts and hot spots of Morocco, Algeria, Tunisia and Libya, at least. I often wondered how many fell for it.

It had to happen. There was a killing right there on the dance floor over, who else but a girl. The place closed down. Several months later, it burned to the ground.

The last time I saw it, it was in this pitiful state. Another classic gone.

I asked around down by the docks but nobody knew of another night club in the area. They all said the only ones now were in the flash hotels in town. Forget it!

How could you possibly compare the atmosphere of the La Fayette with chandeliers, gleaming chrome fittings, teak dance floor, sparkling toilets and insufferable, boring, hoity-toity people?

137. The Dip

Does anybody remember the old runway at Fiji yonks ago? If you were looking out the window of the terminal, the old 'egg beater' aircraft would trundle down the strip, then disappear into the 'dip' before reappearing and taking to the air. It must have freaked out anyone unaware of the dip; it caught me first time.

138. Moustaches

One day, we received a memo in our mail boxes with the news that management had given permission, from such and such a date, that moustaches were accepted into the ranks of the cabin crew.

Good news.

Within no time at all, it exploded.

There were Mexican, Clark Gable, Spiv, Bombardier, Bandit, Wyatt Earp, Walrus, Sergeant Major, Errol Flynn — in fact, all types except Hitler's 'toothbrush'. It couldn't last. We looked like a mob of deserters from the Bounty.

The rule was very quickly amended so that only well-groomed moustaches no wider than the corners of the mouth would be tolerated. Suave stewards were back.

139. Hell on Earth

My roster sheet said four days in Nagoya, Japan. I purchased a staff ticket and took my wife along with me.

We decided we would go to Hiroshima the next day and caught the train out there. We visited the area devastated by the atomic bomb in 1945 and then the museum. There are still signs of the explosion to be seen everywhere.

Nearby is the Catholic church built in the old-English style of grey stone, which survived the blast. The priests and parishioners had gathered up thousands and thousands of pieces of broken crockery, cups, bowls, saucers, jugs and plates from around the area and cemented them onto the façade of the church. The sight makes a tremendously unforgettable impact.

We really needed a stiff drink after seeing all that first-hand, and were looking forward to one when we got back to our hotel. We needed a double stiff one with what happened next.

On the fairly crowded train back to Nagoya, we were no sooner seated when the elderly lady opposite stood up and started to berate us, the words in Japanese venomously spat out at us. The people all around were embarrassed (as the Japanese can be), looking everywhere but at us.

We had no idea what we had done to deserve it and had no option but to sit there in stunned silence. She was shaking with obvious contempt, completely out of character for a Japanese person.

At the next station, she turned around to get off, and there was the reason. The left side of her face, head and body bore the after-effects of the full impact of the blast. She would have been about ten years old when the explosion occurred, with a long, full life ahead of her. In a split second it had shattered her normal life and future.

We can only conclude that she thought we were Americans and had a deep abhorrence of anything American — and why not? There was no chance to say we were Australians as she stormed off. Even now we still have great pity for that poor lady.

When the second raid happened, the target was Kokura, but it was clouded over. So, as Nagasaki was clear, that's where they dropped the bomb. Each year, Kokura puts on a festival and invites the citizens of Nagasaki over because they were spared. Everything is free for them at this festival.

*

One of the three best scenic views in Japan is from a small town called Amanohashidate in Kyoto Prefecture. It also has the amazing 'stairway to heaven'. The whole country was in full bloom as it was cherry blossom time, and the views were indeed spectacular as promised. The stairway is connected with an ancient ritual that Japanese travellers come from all over to perform. The stairway itself is a simple set of about twenty stone steps going nowhere, with a platform at the top. The ritual is to ascend the steps, turn around, bend over and look between your legs to see Heaven.

It was amazing to see reserved Japanese women, young and old (some supported by friends and relatives), bent over double with their dresses and skirts raised, peering between their legs.

Everyone who did it came down with smiles on their faces. Did they see Heaven or were they smiling at their foolishness?

My wife and I did it and saw cherry blossom trees and a beautiful view, upside down.

140. The El Paso

Whenever I went to Mexico in the early 1960s, I always went down to Garibaldi Square. This part of the city was very dangerous, day or night, and was pure old-style Mexicano. 'Rough' described it perfectly. Tourists were warned not to go there.

The cantinas had dirt floors and the streets were unpaved. In winter they were muddy and in summer windswept and dusty. The buildings with shuttered windows that surrounded the square were in a sorry state. Cantinas were predominately for macho male drinkers.

The local caballeros wore everyday cowboy clothing complete with guns and bandoliers (several years later guns were banned in public). Gone forever was the bandit look and character. Mariachi minstrels were rough-looking fellows in even rougher costumes, roving around the bars.

If Clint Eastwood, with guns smoking, had burst through the batwing doors, it would not have been out of place. So, I took my wife there. It was still rough, ready and dangerous. I had got to know the doorman of the El Paso Cantina, which I liked. He gave me the nod and we went inside.

'Wow!' my wife, Annette, exclaimed. It could have been a Hollywood western set, except this was the real thing, even up to authentic bullet holes all over the ceiling.

The cantina was crowded with locals, and all eyes were on my wife. They were amazed a 'gringo' would bring his wife here.

A group at a table shuffled over for Annette to sit down. I went to the antique bar to get drinks. I turned around to see her completely surrounded by caballeros with guns on their hips, teeth missing, moustaches, long untidy hair, sombreros, silver buttons down the seams of their trousers, high-heeled boots, one or two with spurs — all grinning at her. We were the only ones in the bar not packing a gun.

My Sydney suburban housewife was completely out of her comfort zone and was loving it. I burst out laughing and bought them all Tequilas. That night still makes us smile, and all those rough men who treated us with such respect as well.

Many years later I went back — dirt roads now cobbled, the cantinas all gone, everything restored, painted and cleaned to the enth degree — UGH! The mariachis were now in tailor-made, spangled outfits, strutting about like peacocks. All the fantastic genuine characters were gone, probably in a push to sanitise the square even further.

Street food stalls selling tortillas, tacos, burritos and menudo stew, along with street vendors selling (I suspect) fake lottery tickets — all got the heave-ho.

Tours now include Garibaldi Square for reasons I can't fathom, as there is nothing authentic to see any more. Adios, El Paso.

141. Gone

Long before tourism overtook and ruined them, countries had romantic names, conjuring up mystique and intrigue — Siam, Java, Rhodesia, Persia, Burma, Congo, Holland, Hellas, Cathay, Ceylon.

Cities also had great names like Peking, Constantinople, Bombay, Rangoon, Saigon, Batavia.

Do such names conjure up visions of tattooed seamen, pirates, people in national dress, coolie hats, rickshaws, beggars, dingy bars, street food stalls, go-downs and street girls? Not anymore.

142. Chop, Chop

Most large companies have a small percentage of smart-alecks. Our airline did — stewards who slipped past the selectors but should never have been employed.

I gave up going anywhere with these idiots very quickly.

They treated bar tenders, restaurant people, taxi drivers and shop assistants appallingly, with never any sign of 'please' or 'thanks'.

'Chop, chop! Hey you, gimmie a beer.'

These same idiots treated our own Chinese catering people in Hong Kong the same way, calling them all 'John', knowing how they hated it.

The climax came when Hong Kong declared that if the practice did not stop immediately, they would refuse to service our airline. Management had a fit. Hooray for Hong Kong and common decency.

143. Haa Toro

There was a Mexican TV commercial in Sydney many years ago advertising Stuyvesant cigarettes. It pictured a man sitting at a table smoking, then the camera pulled back to reveal he was at a bull-fighting stadium in Mexico. It then pulled back even further to show the whole arena and stadium. It was a very good advertisement and I decided one day to try and find that arena.

My adventurous wife was again along with me, so today was the day. We found it — La Morena Texcoco. Wednesday was hot food stalls day at the arena and tables and chairs were set up in the stands. There was a large group of American tourists there for lunch with free wine in porrons, containers like a teapot with a spout for pouring the red wine into your mouth and usually all over yourself. The flies came for the spilt wine and the entertainment began. A few Mexican tunes played by roving minstrels were designed to get you in the mood for what came next.

A matador then appeared in the arena calling for people to come down and try their hand at bullfighting.

My wife put her hand up to my astonishment and they took her down to dress her in the 'suit of lights'. She was on her own. The only one game enough to try.

There was a small shrine there she told me later, and they asked her, 'Would you like to say a prayer like the matadors did before going out?' Then a quick lesson with the cape and she came out into the arena. The silence was deafening. An American woman's voice clearly rang out, saying, 'Gosh, that little gal's got guts.'

The bull was then let out, not full size, and not a calf either, with horns. Annette did four passes with the cape and we could all hear her calling 'Haa Toro' with each pass, then she decided to quit while in front, to enormous applause.

More catcalling greeted her on her return to her seat, with remarks such as 'Atta girl', 'She's some lady' and 'Lemme buy you a drink'.

She has a certificate and photo to prove she did it. Unlike the Spanish, the Mexicans don't kill the bull; it is just a plaything like a football.

144. My Little Trick

I'll let you into a little secret I know. Flying merrily along, doing the cabin patrol, I would see some poor passenger suffering with the dreaded airsickness. If the passenger happened to be wearing clip-on earrings, I would ask the person to take one off.

I carried paperclips in my coat pocket for those without an earring. I would clip one onto the earlobe. It worked in lots of cases in less than half an hour and the passenger went from being as sick as a dog, to eating the meal.

It must have something to do with pressure on the earlobe, or the middle ear, plain hope, or a placebo effect. All I know is, it worked time and time again. Some resisted the idea of having a paper-clip on their ears until it worked for them.

Remember the pirates, Long John Silver, Black Bart Morgan and their trusty crews? They all had one earring. They knew — try it!

145. Dining in the Third World

One day in Bangkok, eating with a mate of mine in a small restaurant, we ordered chicken and chips. You can't mess that up, can you? When it came, I absent-mindedly flicked black specks off the chips. On closer inspection, they turned out to be little legs. I jumped up and pushed through the bead curtain into the kitchen and there was the cook with a fly swat, swatting flies and cockroaches crawling all over the chips.

*

The large ferry that left Guilin each day at midday going down the Li River in China was usually very crowded. I purchased a second-class ticket because that's where the real China is, amongst the chicken coops, pigs, bamboo poles, coolie hats and the characters.

The scenery we glided past was beautiful: the mountains rising straight up in columns, lush rice fields, people tending their fields and livestock, and the river in the foreground.

Unfortunately, the river spoilt the scenic view as it had piles of rubbish flowing past — even a dead cow in murky water. At the stern of the ferry there was a make-shift eating area and servery.

I decided to check out the kitchen before ordering and wandered into the chaotic area. They had a unique dishwasher which you won't see anywhere else. It was a huge cane basket with a lid that they filled up with bowls, cups, plates and utensils. Tying a rope to the handle, they heaved it overboard, dragging it along behind, and churning up the muddy bottom. No lunch today, Brian.

I think the worst experience I ever had was in Cairo, again in what appeared to be a very clean, small eatery. Jane, the flight hostess, and I ordered beef curry. Sounded good.

Halfway through and enjoying it, Jane looked up startled and said, 'We're leaving now.' She stood up and took off, me following and ignoring the commotion going on behind us. Yeah, we did a runner and I didn't as yet know why.

Arriving breathless back at the hotel, she told me she had found a finger in the curry. How does a bloody finger get into a curry? Two or three brandies, gargled first, didn't make us feel at all any better.

How would my instructor back in the steward-training school have classed this one — 'horrific'? Over the years it makes me wonder or shudder at just what the crews could have eaten.

146. The Hunter

When we were in the training school, Mr Walton repeatedly warned us that a passenger's view on religion, politics, culture, colour, or anything else was never to interfere with service to them. NO MATTER WHAT. I adhered to this rule for thirty years ... except ...

Passengers were boarding at Harare Airport, Zimbabwe. The first-class cabin was only half full and one of the last first-class passengers to board was a hunter. This was obvious by his dress: wide-brimmed felt hat with a leopard-skin band tilted at just the right angle, safari suit complete with a row of loops for bullets, a leather belt contributed by some poor animal, and high-heeled, snake-skin boots.

Strutting up to his seat at the very front (I wonder if that was pre-arranged for his performance?), he turned around and proudly announced for all to hear that he had shot a lion.

Instant hate and horror were on all the passengers' faces, including mine and Robin's, the senior flight hostess. Looking at him made my blood boil. Mr Walton's warning vanished.

'I just physically can't serve him,' I declared. 'You will have to do it, Robin.'

'I can't either,' she replied, in tears for the poor lion. 'We will probably both get demoted or sacked.'

'I don't care,' I growled.

Fortune shined on us that day as, no sooner were we airborne, HE became airsick and was ill all the way to Mauritius where he got off. There was no strutting this time. And no paper clip on the ear for him!

147. The Upside-down Newspapers

Walking about in the suburban streets of Fukuoka in Japan where we stayed for three, and sometimes four, days, I often thought how great it would be to see inside the houses and the manner in which the residents lived. Little did I know.

Newspapers on the Japanese trips were loaded into the first-class cabin as were The Sydney Morning Herald and Asahi Shimbun.

If there were any left over, I would gather up the Japanese papers and take them into the economy-class cabin, like a paper boy.

Holding the papers up high, I passed a Japanese couple smiling behind their hands. I stepped back and asked them what was so funny. With their hands they made circling motions. I was holding the papers upside-down.

This simple mistake has led to a lasting friendship — and seeing inside many homes. 'Why are you coming to Sydney?' I enquired. 'We are on our honeymoon,' he proudly said. Their names are Atsuko and Kasuke Nishida. His very pretty wife asked, 'Have you any suggestions what to do and see?'

'Would you like to go to a barbecue?' I asked. They jumped at the chance.

Annette and I picked them up at their hotel and we

drove up to West Head. They were astounded that so many of our family members were there, playing cricket, badminton and barbecuing. They fitted in just fine.

We showed them the usual things: Manly, a ride on the ferry, the zoo, Harbour Bridge, Opera House and Bondi — but the thing they often brought up in conversation even years later was that barbecue in the bush. Another thing that impressed them greatly was when we took them to dinner at the local RSL, where, at 6 o'clock, everybody stood up, faced the west with a two-minute silence, and the Ode of Remembrance was played. I could see their minds thinking, WHY are we not doing the same thing? They stayed with us years later at our house one Christmas time, again with all our relatives.

Later, Annette and I stayed at their house. During the traditional Japanese dinner, sitting awkwardly on cushions on the floor at a low table, I casually asked Kasuke what his father did before he passed away. There was complete silence and their eyes were downcast. I had blundered into a no-no area.

Kasuke's mother, Chisuko, stood up, politely bowed to us and left the room. Kasuke quietly told me his father had been a captain during the naval battle of Midway in the Pacific, but would not say anymore. Annette and I were both alarmed that our friendship was possibly over and that there was no way back.

At least an hour went by before Chisuko came back into the room carrying a wooden box about sixty centimetres long and tied with a tasselled, yellow cord. She knelt down in front of us, bowed and held out the box with both hands for us to take.

Kasuke solemnly indicated for us to open the box with the family nervously watching our reaction. Japanese custom usually dictates that a gift not be opened in front of the giver. Undoing the cord and lifting the lid of the box, we found inside a gilt-edged parchment scroll. It was six-feet long with beautifully calligraphed script in Japanese. This is what Chisuko had been doing for the past hour.

We had no idea what it said, and they didn't enlighten us so we just accepted it graciously. The mood then reverted to normal. On returning home, I hung the scroll in the study, and when our daughter, Angela, who speaks and writes Japanese, came over, she said to us, 'Do you have any idea what that scroll says?'

'No,' we replied.

'It states that the Nishida family were appalled and ashamed at the atrocities that were meted out to the Australian soldiers in World War II, and the family begs our forgiveness.'

We had — and have never told them — two uncles on the Burma Railway.

Kasuke told me some time later that they had wanted to express their feelings but could not find a way. My innocent enquiry about his father created the opportunity. We have remained good friends for over forty years.

148. Devastated

As they say, time flies when you are having fun. And so it was with my flying career — and retirement age loomed up all too fast.

At the Sydney Mascot airline base, overlooking Kingsford Smith Airport, standing there like a stunned mullet in the same office where I had had several dressing-downs, I was now shaking hands with management, personnel officers and roster clerks, all saying, 'thank you', 'good luck' and 'farewell'.

What really shattered me most was when I handed in all my equipment and uniforms, the clerk carelessly gathered them up in his arms, turned around and dumped the lot in the bin. With it went a lifetime of memories and experiences.

Leaving the office, I walked over to the chain-wire fence at the end of the runway in the bright sunshine and watched several 'flying machines' thunder overhead.

Who was now sitting in my take-off seat? It was devastating! I wondered what would become of me.

The second day home after walking through the airline security gates for the last time, I was standing in the kitchen, gazing into space when my wife Annette turned around and bumped into me yet again.

In exasperation, she blurted out, 'It's like having a grand piano in the kitchen.

149. The End — but also the beginning

Sister Helen, a local Catholic nun gave me singing tuition in her choir, and two years later this small group of eleven was invited to sing in St Peter's Basilica in Rome. Afterwards, His Holiness singled me out to shake my hand. I've shaken hands with a saint!

This was followed by my wife and I taking up dancing at Tamworth, NSW. We both took out the national Australian championship, winning a gold medal.

I joined the local vintage car club and over a period have owned an array of vintage cars with which I enjoy tinkering. I have kept my faithful old Wolseley, which I have had for nearly sixty years. It was my transport to and from the airport for all those years with the front bucket seat removed for my flight bag and suitcase. If I gave anyone a lift home, he or she had to sit in the back.

Life really does go on, but it's not nearly as adventurous and exciting as the best job in the world. Would I do it all again?

Yes, yes, yes.

www.ingramcontent.com/pod-product-compliance
Lightning Source LLC
Chambersburg PA
CBHW041136110526
44590CB00027B/4040